CW00661550

# THE FIRST PRINCIPLES OF

# PIANOFORTE PLAYING

# THE FIRST PRINCIPLES OF
# PIANOFORTE PLAYING

BEING AN EXTRACT FROM THE AUTHOR'S

## "THE ACT OF TOUCH"

DESIGNED FOR SCHOOL USE, AND INCLUDING
TWO NEW CHAPTERS

## DIRECTIONS FOR LEARNERS

AND

## ADVICE TO TEACHERS

BY

TOBIAS MATTHAY

BOSWORTH & CO. LTD.,
14/18 HEDDON STREET,
REGENT STREET,
LONDON, W 1

LOWE AND BRYDONE PRINTERS LTD
VICTORIA ROAD, LONDON, N.W 10

# PREFACE.

This little work is issued to render the teachings of "The Act of Touch" better available for the School-room and Class-room, and as a Text-book for Examinations. It is intended as an Introduction to the subject.

The supreme importance of early training in this subject—the mechanism of playing—need not be further dilated upon here, since it has been proved that Agility itself, and all those contrasts of Tone and Duration which enable us musically to express ourselves through the Pianoforte, depend immediately on the proper fulfilment of the laws of Touch, the polemics of which have been amply dealt with in "The Act of Touch."

This "Introduction" consists of the promised "Extract" from the original work, from which I have drawn the Preface and a selection from its Recapitulatories and Summaries. To these selections I have added two new and important Chapters : "*Advice to Teachers and Self-teachers,*" and "*Directions and Definitions for Learners.*" This last Chapter roughly covers the whole ground. It is intended for those beginning the study of Touch, and I have endeavoured to couch it in language simple enough to fit it even for children.

Its study—accompanied by constant experiment at the keyboard—should be followed by the perusal of the "Extract"; taking this in the following order: (1) the final Summary and

v

Conclusion; (2) the Summaries of the four Parts; and (3) the Recapitulatories of the Chapters of each of these Parts.

Constant reference to the "Directions for Learners" should accompany subsequent Practice.

Students sufficiently earnest and intelligent to desire more detailed information should follow this, by study of the "Advice to Teachers," and of "The Act of Touch" itself; first referring to the "Contents" of its Chapters, and finally to the text of these.

The flattering reception accorded to the parent work leads me to hope that this, its offspring, may prove even more directly helpful alike to Teacher and Pupil. The promised extra Part, "*Relaxation*—Exercises in Muscular-discrimination," is also in preparation.

The second Edition is a reprint of the first, except that some slight misprints have been corrected, and some additions made to pages 1, 126, 129, etc.

TOBIAS MATTHAY.

HAMPSTEAD, LONDON.

# CONTENTS

\* N B —The page-references found in this " Extract " apply to "The Act of Touch "

# DIRECTIONS AND DEFINITIONS FOR LEARNERS.

## SECTION I.

### HOW TO TREAT THE KEY:

§ 1. Regard the Pianoforte as consisting of two distinct portions· (I) *the instrument itself*, which can be made to sound—being the Strings and connected Sounding-board, and (II) *the machine*, or Tool, by which it is made to sound—being the KEY and its mechanism, ending with the felt-covered hammer.

§ 2. When you move the key down, its other (hammer) end tilts up ' like a see-saw, and in rising it gives up to the String any *motion* which you may have succeeded in imparting to the key while you were moving your end of it down.*

§ 3. The hammer reaches the String when your end of the key is *nearly* down, and the mechanism allows the hammer *to fall back* at that very moment  Any motion you wish to give the String through the hammer must therefore be imparted to it *before* that moment.

§ 4. You can best become aware of that moment by *listen-* ᴠ *ing* for it, for it is the *beginning* of the sound.

Anything you do to the key after that moment cannot possibly help to *make* the sound in any way.

§ 5. The strings will however continue sounding (more and more faintly) until you let the key rise, when the descend. ing Damper at once stops the sound.

---

¹ An Upright, unlike a Grand piano, has its strings placed upright, hence the hammer itself moves horizontally to reach the strings  Nevertheless the hammer-end of the *key* (and connected mechanism) does " tilt up " just as in the case of the Grand-action

* Listen for this moment.

1

§ 6. The *louder* you want a note to be, the more *swiftly* must you make the key move during its descent.

§ 7. If you want the sound to be beautiful in quality, you must set Key and String *gradually* into motion—however great the swiftness required at the last moment of key-descent.

§ 8. Whereas, if you want a less beautiful but more incisive and "brilliant" tone, you may depress the key *suddenly,*—you may then *hit* the String *by means* of the key, but still taking care not to hit the key instead.

§ 9 If the sound is to be *exactly what you want* as regards tone-amount and tone-quality, you must be careful not only to direct your effort wholly to the sound, and to that only, but you must also succeed in choosing that effort, rightly, for each note.

This you can only do, by actually *feeling* how much the key resists being moved.

§ 10. Since you must be able to judge Key-resistance, it follows that you must always *reach the key gently* This you may do at the moment that you want the key to move down, or you may do so beforehand.

In this way, as you meet the key, and while you are moving it, you can judge its resistance, and can thus accurately judge how much force is required and how to use it.

§ 11. You will now understand why it is wrong to squeeze the key upon the "bed" beneath; for if you do so, you cannot "aim" your effort *to the sound* only. If you commit this error, your effort (chosen for a particular inflection of tone as it should be) will be partly spent upon the key-beds instead of *upon the strings;* hence the result thus obtained cannot represent the effect you intended; and your playing must hence sound *un-musical*, because the result is un-meant.

"Key-bedding" also tires your hands and fingers Likewise, it prevents AGILITY, since it impedes your passage across the keyboard; and in the same way ruins your Staccato, since the key cannot then be free to *rebound*, as it should be for Staccato.

§ 12. The two chief rules of Technique (as regards the Key) are therefore:

(a) Always *feel* how much the Key resists you—feel how much the key "wants" for every note, and (b) always *listen* for the moment each sound *begins*, so that you may learn to direct your effort to the sound only, and not to the key-bed.

If you have succeeded in these two respects, you will have successfully judged each note both *musically* and *instrumentally*, and you will have made considerable progress towards playing musically.

§ 13. You will now understand the following General Directions·

**You must never hit a key down, nor hit *at* it.**      **The finger-tip may fall upon the key—and in gently reaching the key, you may follow up such fall, by acting against the key. This action against the key must be for the sole purpose of *making it move*—in one of those many ways which each give us quite a different kind of sound. And you must always therefore *direct* such action to the point in key-descent *where sound begins***

**In short: (a) If you hit the key, you cannot feel it, and cannot then tell *how much* it requires doing to; and (b), if your action is *too late* during key-descent, you cannot then obtain the exact sound you intend, nor any ease in playing.**

§ 14. The following little SUMMARY OF THE CHIEF FACTS AS TO THE KEY will now prove useful  Fix these facts well in your mind, otherwise subsequent study of the Muscular-facts will prove useless.

**a): It is only by making the hammer-end of the key move, that you can make sound.**

**b): The swifter that movement, the louder the sound.**

**c): The more gradually this swiftness is obtained, the more beautiful is the quality of the sound.**

**d): For brilliant tone, you may hit the String by means of the Key, but do not by mistake hit at the key instead.**

**e): You must "aim" the key to the *beginning* of each sound, because the hammer falls off the string as you**

hear that beginning, and it is too late then to influence the sound, except as regards its mere continuation.

f): It is wrong to squeeze the key-beds, because it prevents tone, impairs musical-result, impedes Agility,
and is besides fatiguing.

g): You must feel the "giving-way point" of the key, so
that you may be able to tell how much force is required for each note. Never therefore really hit the
keys.

---

## SECTION II.

### CONCEPTS OF TOUCH:

### THE DIFFERENCE BETWEEN STACCATO AND LEGATO, HOW IT SHOULD BE PRODUCED AND CONCEIVED:

§ 15. To obtain Staccato, you must allow the key to *rebound*, otherwise the damper will not descend sharply enough
to prevent the prolongation of the sound.     It is not enough
merely to allow the key to rise *soon after* the sound is reached;
on the contrary, you must so carefully time the cessation of
your action against the key, that the key *jumps back* like a ball,
and brings your finger up with it, in its rebound.

§ 16  If you want the sound to continue (Tenuto or Legato),
then you must allow sufficient Weight to continue resting on
the key to keep it down.  But *you should not* use more Weight
*continuously* on the key than will just suffice to sound the
key softly.  The weight left on the keyboard *between* the successive notes in Legato, should therefore be quite light, even
when you have to use much energy and weight *during* key-
descent to obtain a *forte*.

§ 17. Realise now, that in playing a loud note either Tenuto
or Legato, you have really to do *two* different things·—(1) you
must use sufficient energy to make the key move down swiftly
enough to obtain that *forte,* and while you must *stop* using most
of this energy the moment the hammer reaches the string, you
must nevertheless (2) *continue* using some little remnant of
energy (just sufficient Weight) to keep the key depressed.

§ 18. Next recognise· that such a combination also applies to running passages taken Staccato; for unless you also rest on the keys in Staccato, you can neither feel where the keys are, nor how much force they require to move them.    But this continuously-resting weight must be lighter than in Legato. It must be so light that it does *not* compel the fingers to continue holding their keys down.   And if you want Staccato, you must also be careful to remember the rule given in § 15—to leave the Key free to rebound.

§ 19  In fact, you now see that this process of "Resting" can be of two kinds, and that it forms the physical difference between Staccato and Legato·—

(1) In Staccato, the "Resting" must continue at the *surface-level* of the keyboard—for the keys will then be instantly free to rebound, provided you accurately time the cessation of each key-depressing action.

(2) In Legato or Tenuto, the "Resting" must be very slightly heavier, but not more so than just suffices to compel the finger to retain its key depressed

§ 20  Realise meanwhile, that the something you do to each key during its flash of descent must be *different* for each kind and degree of sound. We call this short-lived act "the Added-impetus," because it is added to the "Resting." Always remember that the duration of this "Added-impetus" must in no case be longer than in the shortest Staccato,—it must cease the moment that sound is reached in key-descent.

## PIANISSIMO WEIGHT-TOUCH AND THE TENUTO-RESTING :

§ 21. The force or weight required to keep a key depressed in Tenuto or Legato (*vide* § 16) is very slight indeed   You can tell how slight, if you carefully *weigh* the key down.   To do this, you must allow your *whole arm* to relax (from the shoulder) until the key is just overbalanced, and in giving way thus, it sounds at its very softest   You here realise how slight is the force required to retain a key depressed.

§ 22. Notice that in thus learning to weigh keys until they as it were "slide down" under you, you have also learned to produce one of the most valuable effects available from the instrument, and that is the true *pianissimo,* for in thus over-balancing the keys you are producing the very softest sound possible from them.

This most delicate of all "Weight" touches is important for several reasons —

     a) It enables you to play Legato with ease and certainty.

     b) It enables you to play really *ppp.*

     c) It teaches you to judge Key-resistance, and thus enables you also to judge how much more effort will be required for any greater tone.

§ 23. Notice also, that in thus weighing a key down at its softest, you are doing only *one kind of thing* before, during, and after Key-depression; and that this is therefore the only kind of "*simple*" Touch. All other touches are "*compound,*" as we have seen in §§ 17 and 18, for in them you find that the *something* you continue to do after the key is down is quite different from the something you do to make it go down.

### THE STACCATO-RESTING:

§ 24. The weight employed for the Staccato "Resting," should be the weight of the Hand alone, left loosely resting on the keys.[1] This, though insufficient to compel the fingers to retain their keys depressed, does serve to tell you *where* they are; and you can in this way rest continuously on the key-board *at its surface level,* nevertheless obtaining a perfect Stac-cato,—always provided that you carefully "aim" and cease each tone-making impulse.[2]

§ 25 You see therefore (as pointed out in § 19) that the

[1] When the hand lies released on the keys, it is only *half* its whole weight that can take effect upon the keys—since its wrist-end is supported by the arm. The whole weight of the hand of course becomes available when the arm itself is relaxed. Release of the shoulder helps arm-weight in the same way

[2] The following makes this clear:

a) The Resting ·

b) Tone-producing Impulse :

aa) At *Surface*-level

bb) Aimed towards Tone emission.

cc) The 'Key-bed" surface.

Some residue of force is bound to reach the key-beds at cc)—beyond the tone-producing climax at bb).

difference between natural Staccato and Legato (or any inflection of Tenuto) depends on this slight difference in the Weight
applied during the "Resting";—in the first case allowing the
fingers to rebound with the key, and in the second case com-
pelling them to retain then keys depressed

## LEGATO—TENUTO-RESTING TRANSFERRED:

§ 26. To obtain the effect of Legato, you must learn neatly
to transfer the heavier Resting-weight from key to key. This
transfer of weight from finger to finger is exactly like *walking* —
You must cause the weight to pass on to each next finger, not
by trying to *do* something with that "next" finger, but by
carefully timing the last-used finger to *stop* the slight work it
is doing in supporting the continuously-resting weight. That
is: you must carefully stop using the last finger *at the very
moment* that you want the weight to "pass on" to the next
finger. The transfer of weight will then seem *to do itself*, and
the Legato will then seem "natural"—because semi-automatic.[1]

The slighter weight allowed to rest on the surface of the
keyboard in Staccato is transferred from key to key in the same
way.

## SECTION III.

### HOW WE SHOULD USE OUR ARMS, HANDS AND FINGERS

§ 27. You have perceived how necessary it is constantly
to *weigh* and *judge* the resistance of the keys, and how the
*pianissimo* requires that same process   You must now at
once learn to do this at the keyboard·—

Place several finger-tips upon the keys—upon the
\   notes forming a triad is best, first of all. Now relax

---

[1] Here re-read §§ 16, 17 and 18, also 21.

your *whole* arm gradually until the keys give way, and
they sound without your seeming to "do" anything
In this way you learn to weigh the keys exactly in the
same way that you weigh or "balance" any other object.
You can learn to do this balancing so neatly, that (for
the sake of practice) you can even succeed in swaying
the whole arm (from the shoulder) up and down *with
the keys*, meanwhile *not* taking them down far enough to
sound them [1]

In any case, you must not rest satisfied until you succeed
in *letting the keys tell you* with certainty the least amount of
weight they require to make them sound at their softest through
being thus weighed down. To succeed in this, you must give
your attention to the key itself; you must not think of your
arm, but you must try to feel "how much the keys want."

§ 28. In thus weighing the keys, you are aware that you
are using Arm-weight, and that this reaches the keys *through*
the finger and hand    Particularly notice now, that your finger
and hand must therefore be doing something; in fact that
you have to *exert* them very slightly (but sufficiently) to *support* this slight arm-weight upon the keys    It is difficult at
first to realise that this is so, as the whole combination of exertion and weight is so slight in this case.

§ 29. Try to understand next, that your finger, in thus
acting *downwards* upon the key to support the weight, *also
re-acts upwards* against the knuckle of the hand, and that it
does so with exactly equal force    The hand itself, moreover,
is also exerted *downwards* at the Knuckles, and it in turn again
re-acts *upwards* against the arm at the Wrist-joint, and thus
supports the arm there [2]

If you succeed in thinking this out, you will learn, that all
exertion made during the Act of Touch must *feel upwards—*
and not downwards as you might at first expect    The exertions must *feel* upwards (by re-action from the keys), because

---

[1] The movement should be but slight , and the fingers and hand must of
course not fail to convey the Weight upon the keys.    *Vide* § 28.

[2] Remember, these exertions are very slight indeed in *pp*

those of the finger and hand are the ones you should mostly use—*between* the keyboard and the arm, at the wrist.

In walking, standing, or running, you have a similar effect · It is true that your feet press upon the ground, but the exertion is *upwards*. And the moment you feel at the Piano as if you were acting *downwards*, you may be sure you are employing the wrong exertions.

§ 30. The more weight you let loose, at the moment of sounding the note, the more can the finger and hand thus *act* against the key, and the louder will the sound be.

§ 31 You will now have realised, that it is *three* different things you have been applying against the key to make it move. viz :

a) The *weight* of the arm.

b) The *exertion* of the hand, and

c) The *exertion* of the finger.

Now, when you thus make the key move by using all these three things *together*, we call this muscular combination.—

THE THIRD SPECIES OF TOUCH.

§ 32. But you must not always use this Third Species. In place of this *third* Species, you can do without Arm-weight. while producing the sound by only using the exertions of the finger in conjunction with those of the hand.

That is: you can prevent the arm from lying on the keys through the fingers, by keeping it *supported by its own muscles;* and can still cause the keys to move by a greater or lesser exertion of the fingers and hand alone— the arm meanwhile as it were *floating* over the keyboard.

In thus making sound by exerting the finger and hand, but without the assistance of relaxed arm-weight, we obtain.—

THE SECOND SPECIES OF TOUCH.

§ 33 Again, in place of this Second Species, we can even do without the exertion of the hand, and can produce the sound by finger-exertion only.

B

That is: while causing the arm merely to "float'
over the keys, as in Species II, you may let the hand
*lie loosely* upon the keys, and may then use the finger
alone against the key to move it.

This combination we call:—

THE FIRST SPECIES OF TOUCH.

§ 34. Be sure to understand the difference between these
three alternative muscular-*combinations*, for you will find they
each have their place in Music. To sum up this matter, remember that you can make the tone either by·

*First Species*. Finger alone exerted against key, in
combination with loose-lying hand, and self-supported
arm

*Second Species* Hand excited "behind" finger, with
self-supported arm.

*Third Species* · Arm-weight lapsed afresh behind hand
and finger for each note

§ 35. Note in this connection, when the arm is in the "self-supported" state, that it should never be held in the least rigidly,
but that it should be just in a balanced state—almost falling
of its own weight; so nicely balanced that it will be set into vibration by the reiterated actions of the finger and hand.

## AS TO CHOICE OF TOUCH-SPECIES:

§ 36. Note now the following facts:

a) The First Species will enable you to move quickly
across the keyboard, but you cannot obtain much tone
by its means.

b) The Second Species gives a larger range in tone- ⤳
*amount* but reduces your Agility-power

c) The Third Species gives you the full range in tone-amount, but you cannot apply it in very quick passages.

## AS TO MOVEMENTS OF FINGER, HAND AND ARM:

§ 37. You must next learn to understand what is really
meant by the *movements* of the Finger, Hand, and Arm—how
and why they should arise·—

You must consider these three (the finger, hand and arm) to be three separate *levers*—and the arm-lever itself to be available either as Fore-arm only, or as Upper-arm in conjunction with the Fore-arm. Now you have learned that you can *use* these three levers independently of the others in a measure, and you will now see that you can also *move* each one of these three independently of the others. Touch can therefore be *accompanied* by movements of either the finger, hand, or arm, and it is these movement-distinctions that are called Finger-touch, Hand-touch, and Arm-touch, respectively.

§ 38. While learning to recognise these *movement*-distinctions, be most careful not to allow this to confuse you as to those other, and far more important distinctions (as to muscular-STATE), which you have learned to recognise as the Three Species of Touch.

If you have thoroughly grasped the meaning of these "Three Species of Touch" (§§ 31–36) you will now be able to understand what the accompanying *movements* really signify, as follows·—

§ 39 FINGER-TOUCH—when you *move* the finger only during key-descent; this may consist either of:

    a) An exertion of the finger only (First Species of Touch-formation).

    b) An exertion of the hand behind the finger (Second Species of Touch)—but note that it is the finger only which *moves*, although the hand is *active*.

    c) Arm-weight released behind hand and finger (Third Species)—but note again, that the finger alone *moves*, in spite of the *triple* nature of the muscular-combination.

§ 40. HAND-TOUCH (formerly termed "Wrist-touch")—when you *move* the Hand alone during key-descent; this may consist either of·

    a) The combined exertion of the hand and fingers (Second Species)—but without showing any movement of the fingers relatively to the hand, the *hand* therefore alone moving with the key during its descent.

b) Arm-weight lapsed behind the finger and hand (Third
Species)—but the hand alone *moving*.

§ 41 ARM-TOUCH—when you move the arm itself, either
the fore-arm only, or the whole arm; this must consist of Third
Species, for the arm must be relaxed to cause the movement,
and the fingers and hand must also *act* so as to convey this weight
upon the keys, and this in spite of the fact that neither finger
nor hand change their position relatively to the descending
arm during key-descent.

§ 42. Note particularly, that you must allow the Arm to
*fall of its own weight*, rather than exert it downwards.

## AS TO CHOICE OF MOVEMENT:

§ 43. The choice is determined by the speed of the passage:—
a) For slow passages and for the beginnings of phrases,
   it is best to employ arm-movement—"Arm-touch."
b) For quicker passages, choose hand-movement—Hand
   Touch (so-called "Wrist-touch"), since that is less
   clumsy than moving the arm at great speed.
c) For the quickest passages, you must use finger-
   movement only—"Finger-touch." But you may also
   use finger-touch for slower passages; and you must
   of course do so for Legato passages

Again be warned not to confuse these distinctions of Touch
(derived merely from movement) with those far more important
distinctions you have recognised as the three main touch-
formations, or Species of Touch.

## THE CONTRASTS IN TONE-QUALITY—WHAT THEY DEPEND UPON, MUSCULARLY:

§ 44. Differences in Tone-*quality* depend chiefly upon the
fact that you can *start* the act of touch either by *willing Muscular-exertion* or by *willing Weight-release*. Thus:—

When you employ the Third Species, you can *start* that
triple muscular-combination [1] in either of two distinct ways· You

---

[1] The triple combination, of Arm-weight release and the supporting exertions of the finger and hand.

can *start* it (a) by *willing* the hand-and-finger *exertion*, but allowing the arm-*release* to occur in answer to the re-action felt at the
wrist; or you can cause the combination to arise (b) by *willing*
the Arm-release itself, and allowing the finger and hand to act
purely in response to the *weight* felt to be set free—the finger and
hand acting only sufficiently to insure the weight reaching the
key.[1]

> a) If you want bright, incisive, "brilliant" tone, you
> must start the combination in the *first* way;—the
> third Species may then be said to be "muscularly-
> initiated"; in short, it is "Muscular-touch."
>
> b) If you want thick, singing, carrying tone, you must
> start the combination in the *second* way;—and the
> touch is then "weight-initiated," or "Weight-touch."

There is only one way of starting the First and Second
Species;—these touches are necessarily muscularly-*started* since
there is no Weight-release in their case; and the tone-quality
must therefore also tend towards the brilliant type rather than
towards the sympathetic.

Study the above directions most carefully, and remember,
if you want beauty of tone, you *must not allow yourself* to think
of action or exertion. If you properly employ the Weight-
touch, it feels as if the keys "go down of themselves"—for
you must not become conscious of the exertion of the finger
and hand, and you *cannot feel* Weight-release, since it arises
owing to your *ceasing* to act with the arm-sustaining muscles,—
the more completely so, the greater the tone required.

§ 45. While these two different ways of *starting* the muscular
act form the chief difference between thick and thin qualities of
tone, you still have to learn one more distinction, and that is:
the difference between *bent* and *flat* finger—or THRUSTING and
CLINGING methods of touch.

For you can reach the key either:—

> a) With the finger *well bent* beforehand; or
> b) With the finger much flatter or *straighter* beforehand.

---

[1] In short —In the one case you *start* at the Finger-and-hand end, levering
the released Arm-weight on to the key, while in the other, you *start* with
Arm-lapse, using the hand and finger in response.

Now if you reach the key in the first way (from a well-bent position), your finger will *thrust* against the key, and this will greatly help to induce the sharper or more brilliant kind of tone.

Whereas, if you reach the key from a flatter (or more opened-out) position of the finger, your finger will act upon the key in a *clinging* way, and this kind of key-attack will greatly help you towards the *singing* kind of tone.

§ 46. Before going to the Piano with this information, you must however notice that this difference between the "thrusting" and "clinging" finger demands two quite opposite states of the *upper-arm*—and Elbow, therefore.—

    a) For the Bent-finger attitude, you must be careful not to suffer the Upper-arm (Elbow) to lapse, as this would spoil the thrusting action of the finger. Although the *fore-arm* may in some cases be allowed to help slightly.

    b) For the Flat-finger attitude, the relaxation of the Upper-arm must correspond to the force the finger exerts in clinging upon the key during its descent.

In fact, it is this difference in the state of the Upper-arm (whether relaxed or not) which should be the real cause of the difference between the two finger-methods. The anticipated fall of the upper-arm causes one to use the finger in the clinging or "grabbing" way; while the consciousness of the forward-sustained Elbow causes one to direct the fingers in a kind of stamping or thrusting action.

§ 47. Singing-tone, you will now see, is obtained when you employ the Third Species in its Weight-started form *in conjunction with* the Clinging-finger (and Arm) attitude.

When trying to apply this to the keyboard, do not forget the rules you learned in §§ 7, 9, and 10, etc.; viz.: that key-speed must be gradually obtained when you want beauty of tone, and that all the energy *meant* for the sound must be applied *before* you really reach the sound in key-descent. Realise, therefore, that the weight must *increase* during key-descent, while it must *disappear* the moment you hear the sound,—except-

ing that slight residue to hold the key down, when that is required.

## THE CHANGES IN THE STATE OF THE FORE-ARM IN A ROTARY DIRECTION:

§ 48. It is now imperative that you should understand the
*rotary* alternations in the state of the Fore-arm. For you cannot
alternately exert the thumb-side of the hand and the little-
finger side of it with an equal degree of force, unless you alternately relax and exert the Fore-arm in a *rotary* direction.

§ 49. When you allow this change in the state of the Fore-
arm actually to cause a twisting of it upon itself (thus tilting
the hand either towards the little finger or towards the thumb)
then this act of touch, thus accompanied by a *visible* rocking
motion, is called "*rotation-touch.*"

But you can also alter the state of the Fore-arm in these
directions *without* any such movement being shown, and you
can help the fingers thus in producing tone, without any visible
movement accompanying the *constant change* required in this
way. Thus:—

> You can *support* either side of the hand by means of
> rotary *exertion*, while nevertheless showing no tilting
> movement; in which case there will be nothing at the
> side of the hand *held off the keys* for the fingers *at that
> side* to re-act against, and these will consequently feel
> "weak"; but the fingers at the opposite side will gain
> greatly, for you can either let them have Weight (to
> help them towards a singing tone), or you may help
> them by exerting the fore-arm rotarily in their direc-
> tion (when you require brilliance or "passage-touch")

Hence, if you want to act strongly with the fingers at one
side of the hand, you must be careful to *release* the fore-arm
rotarily in their direction, or even to *exert* it rotarily to help
them. Anyway, you must be careful not to allow any rotary
action of the fore-arm to keep energy *away* from the side of the
hand *where it is required.*

You are very likely to confuse a partial down but *sideway* action of the fore-arm for the true *rotary* exertion; try at once to distinguish between the right and the wrong exertions in this respect: With the true Rotary-exertion (or lapse) there is no displacement of the wrist when rotary movement is allowed to arise,—the wrist merely revolves partially on its own axis to a smaller or greater extent, like the axle of a wheel.

We must clearly realise that visible or invisible rotatory exertions or relaxations are required practically for every note we play. The *direction* of this exertion or relaxation is determined by the position of each playing finger relatively to the hand when compared with that of the finger *last* used. In a word, the necessary short-lived rotatory change is always towards the required finger and *from* the direction of the finger last used, and this applies even when a finger is turned over the thumb, and *vice versa*, the rotatory adjustment is in the nature of an *exertion* when the progression is towards the thumb side of the hand, and is a *relaxation* when it is towards the little finger side of the hand. The principle applies everywhere, even in learning our first five-finger exercise, even in playing a single unbroken octave with one hand; for the natural position of the hand (*minus* rotatory exertion) is side-ways—with the thumb upwards. *See* the author's pamphlet on "The Rotation Element and its Mastery" (Joseph Williams)

## THE AUTOMATIC CESSATION OF WEIGHT:

§ 50. You have learned (§ 26) that for Legato the second or heavier form of "Resting" must be transferred from finger to finger, making this transfer occur by carefully ceasing the supporting action of the finger last used, and timing this last-used finger to "give way" at the very moment you want the new finger to *start* its key-depression;—the previously used finger thus leaving the Resting-weight "in the lurch," and the Legato consequently as it were "doing itself," or becoming almost automatic.

You must next learn, also to *cease* the operation of the Weight used in Species III in a similarly *automatic* way. For you must be careful not to try to *take the weight off* when you reach sound in key-depression; on the contrary, you must leave the weight "in the lurch" by carefully timing *the exertion of the finger and hand to cease* as you reach sound, and you will find that the arm will then automatically save itself from falling— the supporting-muscles of the arm will come into operation unconsciously. If you succeed in thus causing the arm to re-support itself owing to its suddenly being "left in the lurch" at the Wrist, it will seem as if the weight *disappears of itself* when you reach sound, and it will seem as if weight and wrist both "fall through" the sound. Also, after the completion of the act of tone-production, the arm will be found to be re-supported by itself, either completely so, in Staccato, or almost completely so in Legato-Resting.

§ 51. This *timing* of the cessation of Weight and Exertion, is one of the most important things you have to learn, and to keep in practice when learned. This you can easily achieve, by practising the *second* of the Three chief Muscular Tests every day, before practising anything else.[1]  In this way you can learn (and remind yourself) accurately to *aim* the required muscular-operation against the key, and at the same time learn at once to recognise the key-weight and depth of any instrument you are playing upon—and any key of it.

§ 52. Another great muscular difficulty, always more or less in our way, is, that in trying to use our fingers and hands alone, we are very likely *also to force the arm downwards*—an exertion we should always shun so far as possible.

To perfect yourself here, you should every day practise the *third* of "Three Muscular-Tests", this will greatly help to remind you of this necessary *separation* of arm-down-exertion from that of the finger and hand, as required in Species II.

For, until you are able to provide this particular "muscular-discrimination" you will be unable to obtain either a good Staccato, or good Agility.

§ 53. Finally, it is difficult to use one's fingers and hands as *freely* as one should, and here again we can be greatly helped by daily practice of another of these "Three Tests"—the *first* one; for this will teach you to make the necessary exertions *without* these being impaired by contrary exertions of the opposite muscles.

§ 54. Besides these three chief Tests, you should also practise others, such as for Rotary-freedom of the fore-arm, and for freedom in those lateral (side-to-side) movements of the hand

[1] *Vide* Recapitulatory of Chapter XVIII., "The three muscular-tests"

and wrist which are required to facilitate the turning under
and over of the thumb and fingers; both these forms of freedom
being imperative, even if you wish to play a simple scale or
arpeggio with *evenness* [1]

## AS TO MOVEMENTS BEFORE REACHING THE KEYS:

§ 55. As this matter often proves puzzling, a few words
must here be devoted to this detail:

Movements required to bring the finger-tips into contact
with the key-surface do not, strictly speaking, belong to the
Act of Touch itself, since that does not commence until the key
is reached. Ample preliminary movements are however helpful,
when there is time for them. In making such ample movements
with the fingers, we are more likely to learn to use these freely
(provided we are not tempted into hitting at the keys), and we
shall be better able to learn to distinguish each finger from the
others; while in the case of arm-touch, a preliminary movement
of it helps to overcome its *inertia* before the key-surface is
reached, which also is an advantage.

Movements towards the keys, whether of the finger, hand
or arm, should however be *passive* rather than active in their
nature  Thus·—

   a) The Finger, in moving towards a key, should not be
      more exerted than will neatly bring its tip upon the
      key *without any real hitting* of the key-surface. It
      should *almost* fall by its own weight, so slight should
      the exertion be

   b) The Hand, in Hand-touch (so-called "Wrist-touch"),
      should fall of its own weight, if previously raised off
      the key-surface; this suffices in nearly all cases.

   c) The Arm, in Arm-touch, must also be allowed to fall
      of its own weight upon the key, it being however not
      more relaxed than will permit it to fall upon the keys
      comparatively gently, unless a harsh tone is desired.

[1] Exercises for these purposes will be found with others in the "Muscular-
discrimination studies "—"Relaxation studies," Bosworth

Such movement down upon the key, and the true act of touch, subsequent to it, may take the form of a *single and continuous motion;* the required extra force being *added* as the finger-tip touches the key. Or, the key may also be reached at any convenient moment *previously* to this, in which case touch-movement will begin at the key-surface.

## SUPER-LEGATO AND SUB-LEGATO, AND STACCATISSIMO:

§ 56. The inflections of DURATION *beyond* and *below* Legato, and Staccatissimo, are details of Touch which you must presently acquire. Some additional information is therefore necessary:—

### ARTIFICIAL LEGATO, ETC.:

There is an "*artificial*" mode of holding down notes, which is more convenient for certain passages than the *natural* Legato element (the heavier Resting) discussed in § 16, etc.

By giving a very slight but *continuous* exertion of the finger and hand (or the finger alone) you can produce a *slight* tension or "pressure" upon the key-beds; this will enable you to hold down notes thus pressed upon at your Will,—independently therefore of the Resting-weight. This "Pressure-legato element" you can apply either *in addition to* the Legato-resting, or also *in addition to* the Staccato-resting  The resulting effects will be thus —

  a) Pressure applied *in addition to the Legato-resting*, may be used for all inflections of Duration BEYOND Legato, up to the extremest Legatissimo.

  b) Pressure applied *in addition to the Staccato-resting* may be used for all inflections of Duration BELOW the full Tenuto (or Legato) down to Staccato,—when of course it must be completely absent. So-called "Portamento-touch" can also be executed by means of this "pressure-legato," but it requires in addition a tone-production by "Weight-initiative"—§ 44, etc.

In slow successions of notes it is best to obtain both *super-*

legato and *sub*-legato ("semi-staccato") effects by means of increased Resting-weight; but for quick passages it is usually more convenient to employ this "pressure" element [1]

### STACCATISSIMO, ETC.:

Staccato can be rendered slightly more sharp in certain touches by the help of a "kick-off"—a jumping-like action against the key-beds.    You will learn the nature of this *staccatissimo* when practising the *third* of the "Three Muscular Tests." [2]

*More* Resting-weight than usual (in Staccato or Agility) can also be *carried* by the fingers (without its reaching the key-beds) in certain running passages of this nature, provided they are beyond a considerable degree of speed and tone. [3]

§ 57. A short summary of the MUSCULAR FACTS will here be convenient. The following are among the most important points to be kept in mind —

a): The distinction between the two muscular acts (1) the Resting, and (2) the Added-impetus.  That is: (1) the Something which we provide continuously, and which tells us the key's place and its resistance, and (2) the Something we have to do only while the key goes down, and by means of which we produce all tone except the *ppp*. :—

b): In fact, realising: that the momentary muscular action of depressing the key may be vigorous (as in *forte*), while the continuous " Resting " nevertheless remains quite light between the separate tone-makings.

c): The distinction between the two kinds of " Resting," the *first* so light as not to compel the down-retention of the keys— required for Staccato;  and the *second* a little heavier—sufficiently so to compel the retention of the keys in Tenuto and Legato.

---

[1] The greatest CAUTION is imperative when learning to apply this slight tension or "pressure" element, lest you exceed in degree the extremely delicate—almost gossamer-like—pressure required, otherwise it will destroy all Agility, and delicacy of expression.

[2] *Vide* Recapitulatory of Chapter XVIII

[3] *Vide* "Extract". Note on exceptional forms of Legato and Staccato, p 97

d): The importance of eradicating all restraint or stiffness in all the required actions.

e): The nature of the three muscular *components* of Touch, viz.: (1) Finger-exertion, (2) Hand-exertion, and (3) Arm-weight.

f): The three Species of combining these, viz.:—

*I*): The first Species of touch-formation: Finger-exertion only, with loose-lying hand and self-supported arm.

*II*): The second Species of touch-formation: Hand exertion behind the finger, with self-supported arm; and

*III*): The third Species of touch-formation: Release of Arm-weight in conjunction with finger-and-hand exertion.

g): The relationship of *Movement* to these three Species of touch-formation (or *structure*), viz.:

Finger-touch (Finger-movement) may consist of either of the three Species.

Hand-touch [1] (Hand-movement) must consist either of second or third Species.

Arm-touch (Arm-movement) must imply use of third Species.

h): The fact, that all true Agility and *ease* in playing depends on obedience to the two laws: (1) Lightness in Resting (so that we *can* stop working when we reach the sound) and (2) the careful *cessation* of all tone-producing action with the beginning of each individual sound—except in *ppp*.

i): The distinction between Weight-initiated touch and Muscularly-initiated touch—which is the main cause of difference between thick and thin tone-qualities, respectively.

j): The distinction between Clinging and Thrusting touch-methods—which so much enhances the difference between singing and bright tone-qualities.

k): The fact, that the clinging (or flatter) finger requires more or less Upper-arm release; whereas the thrusting (or bent-finger) demands a more or less forward-supported Upper-arm—or Elbow.

l): The great influence of Forearm Rotary-*freedom* in *all* passages, and the rotary *change*, from note to note, nearly always.

m): How the Weight used in Weight-touch should cease to

[1] So-called "Wrist-touch," or "Wrist-action"

operate semi-automatically—owing to the timed cessation of its support at the Wrist.

n) : How the Resting is passed on from finger to finger by a similarly semi-automatic process—owing to the timed cessation of the last-used finger's supporting exertion.

o) : The importance of the three chief forms of muscular-test-ing—(a) for freedom, (b) success in "aiming," and (c) isolation of arm down-exertion from the required finger and hand exer-tions, and other tests.

p) : The subsidary, but still important points, such as the lateral freedom of the hand and wrist; the " artificial " legato element; and the nature of the movements towards the keys, and other details—to be found in the Recapitulatories, etc.

## SECTION IV.

### AS TO POSITION:

§ 58. You must sit far enough from the instrument to enable you to open the arm out sufficiently, else you cannot obtain the advantage of its free weight when required, nor can you move freely across the keyboard.  Do not, however, sit too far off.

§ 59. When you employ the *bent* finger (thrusting-touch) be careful to *start* with it sufficiently bent; the higher the pre-liminary raising the more must it be bent, for the nail-phalange must remain nearly vertical.

§ 60. To enable you to play a scale or arpeggio smoothly, when turning the thumb and fingers under and over, you must let your hand remain more or less turned *inwards*.  For double-notes passages, on the contrary, you must turn the hand in the direction in which the passage is travelling; and when necessary there must be a free side-to-side (lateral) movement of the hand or wrist to enable you easily to accomplish such turning over or under.

§ 61. Do not allow the knuckles to be below the level of the hand when the fingers are depressed with their keys. Also see that the little-finger side of the hand is not lower than the other side; it places the fingers in a helpless position.

§ 62. Keep the thumb well away from the hand; its nail joint should always be in line with its key, except when sounding two notes with it.

§ 63. Except in passages with the thumb on the black keys, the middle-finger should reach its white key in line with the face of the black keys.

§ 64 There are slight changes in the height of the wrist, in passages requiring the thumb alternately on white and black keys; the wrist being very slightly lowered for the black keys The normal position of the wrist should be about level with the hand and forearm.

§ 65. In Staccato, the fingers quit the keys in two different fashions respectively depending on which way they reach the keys—whether in the thrusting or the clinging method.

§ 66. When Hand ("wrist"), or Arm-touches are intended, the fingers should assume their depressed position relatively to the hand before commencing the descent.

§ 67. Above all things: see that each finger is over its note, before commencing the act of tone-production, and that you find the place of each note from the preceding note, or notes, else you will sound wrong notes, or "split" them. See to it, also, that the position *in key-descent*, where the hammer reaches its string, is listened for, and "aimed" for. For it is by means of your "muscular-sense"—the sense of key-resistance, and by your Ear, that you must guide yourself at the Piano; the Eye is of little use—the required movements are too quick for it, and you are likely to restrain them if you try to use it.

§ 68. Carefully study all the foregoing; and to remind you of its main points, read and re-read the following Summary every day, for its Directions apply to every Exercise, Study or Piece you practise or play. When in doubt, refer to the "Extract" and to the "Advice to Teachers," and if you require still further help, refer to the parent work itself: "The Act of Touch."

## GENERAL DIRECTIONS.

a) To make sure of obtaining what you want from the instrument, you must always watch for the "giving-way point" of the keys, so that you can judge how much has to be done to them; meanwhile listen carefully for the beginning of each sound, so that you do not "key-bed".—

b) You must therefore never really hit the key down, nor hit at it. The finger-tip should reach the key-surface gently, and you may follow-up this contact by acting against the key. This action should be for the purpose of making it *move* in one of the many ways which each create quite a different kind of tone. This action you must also always direct to the point in key-descent where sound begins, and not by mistake to the point of key-bed resistance.

c) Remember, if you hit the key, you cannot feel how much it wants doing to, and if your action is too late during key-descent, you can neither obtain the sound you want, nor any Ease in performance.

d) For Singing-tone, do not allow yourself to think of Finger-action or Hand-action. Think of Weight, and use the flat finger too  Everything will then feel elastic.

e) For brilliance of tone, use the sudden "Muscular-touch" instead, and use the bent finger too.

f) If you find it difficult to "get along," or find the passages "sticky," remember, that for Agility you must always (for every note) accurately *cease* all you do to make sound, the moment you reach it, and to enable you thus to "aim" properly, remember you must neither use continuous arm-force, nor even continuous arm-weight·—

g) Weight "off," and careful "Cessation" are the two things that render *Velocity* easy; and you must practise Exercises and Studies, so that you may learn to apply these two laws, and that you may gain Endurance.

h) For Staccato, the rules are the same as for Agility—you

must leave the key free to rebound; it is not enough to let it come back leisurely, it must be left free to bounce back.

i) Natural Legato is easily obtained when you attend to these laws of Agility and Staccato. A little more Resting-weight than for Staccato, is all that is required.

j) Meanwhile, for Evenness and Smoothness, remember the constant application of the changes in the state of the Fore-arm, rotarily—and the necessity of lateral freedom of the hand and wrist.

k) Do not fail to practise the Muscular-tests every day, so long as you mean to keep in playing "form."

## SUMMARY-REMINDER OF MAIN POINTS.

### INSTRUMENTAL:

a): Tone can only be obtained through Key-speed.

b): Beauty of tone through gradual production of the required key-speed.

c): Ability to create key-speed—and String-speed—ceases the moment sound is reached.

d): Key-descent (in its crescendo of force) must be guided to its climax at that point by the Ear.

e): The amount of force must be judged through the Mus-cular-sense from key-resistance itself.

### THE REQUIRED FORM OF ATTENTION:

f): Attention must be given through the muscular-sense to Key-resistance, and through the ear to Sound-beginning.

g): *Key-resistance* is realised through the act of Resting, either in its Legato or Staccato form.

*Sound-beginning* must be definitely timed, and is thus made to agree with the Time (and Tone) felt to be musically due; and this timing thus forms the *union* between Conception and Execution.

c

MUSCULAR:

h): The process of weighing the key, is like ordinary weighing or balancing.

i): The *ppp* is obtained thus, by Weight.

j): Three muscular components are found employed in this process.

k): The third Species of touch is a similar combination, applied only during key-descent, and up to any degree of power.

l): The second and first Species are formed by successively eliminating Arm-weight and Hand-exertion.

m): The distinction between " Muscular " and " Weight " touch.

n): The distinction between clinging and thrusting methods.

o): The two laws of Agility: elision of Arm-force, and accuracy in cessation.

p): The importance of Rotary adjustments.

q): The importance of Ease (non-restraint) in all the required actions.

r): The comparatively unimportant bearing of mere touch-movement (visible " action"), compared to that of Touch-construction—the *state* of the concerned limbs.

THE RULES AS TO POSITION:

s): Distance from keyboard; the bent finger, when raised; the position of the hand laterally, and at the knuckles; Locating keys from preceding keys; etc.

# EXTRACT[1]

## A SELECTION OF RECAPITULATORIES AND SUMMARIES, ETC.

## "THE ACT OF TOUCH"

[1] The page-references in this " Extract " apply to " The Act of Touch."

# PART I.

## *INTRODUCTORY.*

### PREFACE TO "THE ACT OF TOUCH"

ABILITY to understand and feel Music, and ability to communicate such perceptions to others by means of an instrument, are two totally distinct accomplishments. They have often been confused, owing to the fact, that it is impossible to achieve a really satisfactory musical performance without their happy combination.

To become pianoforte players, we must learn Music, and must acquire Taste, but we can only succeed in expressing what we feel, musically, by means of *the physical act of key-depression.* In short, the purely physical act of playing consists solely of an ACT of Touch,—an act of Tone-production. All the gradations of Agility (fleetness of finger), Duration (staccato and legato), as well as all the contrasts of Tone-inflection depend solely and directly on the nature of this act; and it is therefore upon our expertness in the ART of Touch that the whole superstructure of Pianoforte-playing rests. The Art of Touch may indeed be concisely defined as : *command over the Means of Expression.*

This Art thus forms the very Foundation (the Elements or Rudiments) of Pianoforte-playing ; and it can no more be a "gift" (as so often supposed) than is the art of articulate Speech itself ; for it can be acquired by every person of average intelligence. Its precise place in the scheme of Pianoforte Education need not here be further dilated upon, since

Part I. is devoted to that purpose; and the reader is referred to the Summary of this Part, on page 40.

A performer can indeed prove himself to be *musical* only to the extent of his command over touch variety. It is the constant flow of note to note touch-inflections that forces one to realize that a performer is a sentient being. And it is just this Art of Touch, that will for ever defy mechanical imitation; and will for ever render the simplest performance, coloured by human fingers, immeasurably superior to the most complex one obtained by mechanical agency, however perfect the machine.

Although it is only thus, by perfecting himself in the Art of Touch, that the player can obtain the means of expressing his musical sensibilities, yet until within quite recent years the paramount necessity of studying this problem had not begun to dawn upon teachers, artists, and students.

As the true fundamentals of this Art remained practically unrecognized, no serious attempt could be made to give *direct* instruction in it.      True, it was recognised that the musically endowed evinced a "finer touch" than did others less endowed; but this, it was assumed, was owing solely to some occult influence over the keyboard, the possession of which enabled the favoured ones to produce tone of a better quality and of finer gradations,—and there is some half-truth in this, for it is certain that the possession of a musical ear, and a strong wish for musical expression, will undoubtedly compel the player to experiment at the keyboard, until he does sooner or later discover for himself at least *some* of the mechanical Means that will conduce to success.      True, also, that the more serious teachers have insisted upon the necessity of good quality and variety of Touch  But even the greatest, so far, have relied almost exclusively upon empirical methods,

or upon the force of Example. Or they have insisted upon
what is after all a mere *accompaniment* of good touch, i. e. :
Position and Movement—thus placing "the cart before the
horse" True it is, moreover, that the necessity of ra-
tionally studying this problem has lately made itself keenly
felt, especially in America. How pressing this need is, becomes only too painfully evident, when one has to teach those
who have already formed wrong muscular-habits, and when
one is compelled to witness the ineffectual struggles of many
even of the musically endowed in the Examination-room, and
Concert-room, who, were they not thus handicapped by faulty
habits (acquired through ignorance of these Rudiments) could
give free vent to the powers of perception and imagination
evidently latent in them !

Obviously the only way to succeed in the attempt ration-
ally to learn and teach the Act of Touch in all its immense variety, is, first to discover through ANALYSIS how the successful
players obtain their effects, and then to test such Analysis, by
observing whether the *act* of touch, built up in accordance
with such analysis, does give the anticipated tonal-results.
Having thus determined the structure of all varieties of touch,
and the *permits* to Agility, we ought then to be in a position
directly to help ourselves and others towards their acquisition.

The Means of Touch-variety or Key-treatment having thus
been analysed, it follows that all who will take the trouble to
master the subject—all who will take the trouble to understand the requirements of Key and Muscle, and will take the
trouble to form these into physical and mental habits—will
be able to acquire the language of Expression. Everyone
may thus be enabled to gain power of Agility and Colouring ;
and even the musically endowed, may, by *directly* acquiring
a tone-palette (or Touch-palette) thus save years of time, which

would otherwise be wasted in futile experiments, and in forming bad habits.

As I have now for a great number of years applied such
Analysis and Synthesis of Touch in my daily work of teaching,
doing so always with increasing directness, and mainly as-
cribe such success as I have had as a teacher (and my pupils,
also, as teachers) to the resulting ability to point out *the immediate causes of the observed faults*, and the *direct means of their
correction*—to the ability to show explicitly how to command the
physical fulfilment of each interpretative and technical detail, I
have long been urged to render this knowledge more widely
accessible, and the present little work is the result.

In endeavouring to place the many unfamiliar facts and
new ideas before the reader, there was however this dilemma
to face : that innumerable prejudices and fallacies would have
to be combated, and that to do this would render the treatise
too elaborate for the Schoolroom ; whereas, to limit it to direct
information in its concisest form (as required for the School-
room) might render its teachings liable to misconception, and
unacceptable to the prejudiced.

To overcome this difficulty, the work has been laid out in
four Parts, as follows —Part I, is purely introductory, and
purposes to show the relation the study of Touch bears to the
general problems of Pianoforte-education. This is followed
by the practical Parts, II to IV.        Part II, " The instrumental aspect of Key-treatment," demonstrates the nature of
the mechanical difficulties to be overcome,—what are the requirements of the key, and how the key must be treated for
each kind of effect. Part III, " The muscular-aspect of Key-
treatment," exhibits the muscular difficulties of the problem,
and their solution—the muscular means we must adopt, to fulfil the key's requirements. Finally, Part IV deals with the

positional aspect of the subject—the postures and movements which must, or may, accompany correct key-treatment. Each of these practical Parts consists first of a Preamble, giving a general idea of the matter to be dealt with, followed by a number of chapters, providing explanatory details; each of these chapters being followed by a RECAPITULATION, and each of the Parts again by a SUMMARY; the concluding chapter of the work, moreover, giving a Glossary of the whole. A system of Notes accompanies the text, and *Appendices*, which follow each Part, give further opportunity for detailed instruction.

In this way, the close enquirer may obtain full information in the chapters, while the less advanced student can be referred to these Recapitulatories and Summaries. These, in fact, form a work *complete in itself*,—a digest or extract, designed for school use. This Digest or Extract, is intended for publication in a separate form later on, to render it more easily available for such purpose.

The work, it will be seen, is entirely explanatory. It has nothing to do with any particular system of exercises or studies, etc. The *Student* can apply its teachings at any stage of his progress, since it applies in all cases, whatever the system of teaching or exercises adopted in other respects.

The *Artist* can learn from it the reason of his greater or lesser success technically, and how further to improve his powers of Expression. The *Teacher* will find it useful at every step; and finally the *Critic* can find in it a basis for his technical opinions.

This work may presently be followed by an extra Part— Part V, giving certain exercises for acquiring Muscular-discrimination, which have been found useful in direct teaching.

Coming now to the end of the years of labour expended on this little volume, the late Professor TYNDALL'S words recur to me: "The ease with which an essay is read, is often a measure of the laboriousness with which it has been written ; "— and in concluding, I can only express the hope that my readers may find some measure of correspondence between my labour in this instance, and its result!

I must also here take the opportunity of thanking the many kind friends who have encouraged me in my self-imposed task, and to acknowledge the valuable help given me in the revision of the proofs, etc., by Mrs. Kennedy-Fraser, of Edinburgh, and others.

TOBIAS MATTHAY.

HAMPSTEAD, LONDON,
 July, 1903.

THE ACT O

—is accomplished by the uni

---

I:

## CONCEPTION,

—the Perception of Musical Sense.

The power of perceiving musical sense depends on the degree of our

### MUSICIANSHIP

Musicianship the power of understanding Music, has two sides :—

—s

| (a) : | (b) . |
|---|---|
| *The EMOTIONAL SIDE;* and | *The INTELLECTUAL SIDE,* | ARTIS

Emotional Musical-ability, or *Musical-Feeling* permits us to perceive : the *Emotional Import* of Music

It permits us to perceive, and enjoy, the sensuously Beautiful in Music, and its parallelism to Human emotion

Intellectual Musical-ability or *Musical-Reasoning* permits us to perceive : the *Musical-Shapes* employed to convey each emotion.

It permits us to perceive, and enjoy, the perfections shown in the musical structure; workmanship —in its largest and smallest manifestations

It enables us to perceive Rhythmical structure ;— the facts of Climax, or Crisis, in its large swings of form, and in its smaller ones of the Phrase and its subdivisions—down to its component ideas

Artistic-jud edge of, and he instrumer t is alone p sense as one It also emb ity ; a sensib enough to fee even when its rily suspende

---

*Training* is hence required in both the departments, *Conception* and *Execution.* s
Moreover, such Training can only bear fruit, provided ATTENTION is consciou
*This Act of ATTENTION or VOLITION in performance, although apparently*

FOUR

---

MUSICAL attention —*Inwards* —

| (I) · | (II) : |
|---|---|
| *As to TIME;* | *As to TONE;* |
| —*WHERE each note should begin,* | —*HOW each note should sound* |

—An Attention, Judgment and consequent Volition originating from our Musical Feeling and Intelligence provided we insist on these faculties determining the proper mission of each Note,—*as Part of a* WHOLE

The Result to be obtained by such perfect act of Attention and Volition is · that the **PLACING** (both a
The result moreover is  that the Muscular Conditions, necessary to consummate this ‘ *Placing,*” will be
*Firstly,* by our Muscular-sensation—of the key's resistance before and during descent
*Secondly* by our Aural Sensation—of the commencement of tone, arising from the completio

The supr

se particulars becom

# PART I.

AYING

quite distinct acts :—

---

## II:

## EXECUTION;

—the Communication of such perception to others

The power of communicating musical sense, depends on the extent of our

### EXECUTIVE-ATTAINMENTS

Executantship, the power of expressing that which one perceives, has two sides :—

---

(b).

| DGMENT, | and | THE ART OF TONE-PRODUCTION : |
|---|---|---|

mbraces : Knowl
the application of
ts, through which
o translate such
*ive musically*
*isational* sensibil-
ebou'd be keen
rnurnce of Pulse,
ons are tempora-
" *Rubato* "

This implies, *Ability* to obtain from the instrument, every possible kind of tone
of any Quantity, Quality, Duration ; and at any Speed of succession. It embraces
Agility, and Colouring

Adeptness in the Art of Tone-making has two separate aspects :—

| (aa) : | (bb) . |
|---|---|
| *INSTRUMENTAL-KNOWLEDGE,* | and    *MUSCULAR-HABIT* |
| *—Consciousness of what are the require-ments of the Key* | *—Muscular-ability, to fulfil these re-quirements, correctly formed and rapidly retained* |

*Muscular-Habit,* implies two distinct things —

| (aaa) : | (bbb): |
|---|---|
| *Muscular-Discrimination ;* | *Muscular-Application* |
| The power to provide the requisite Muscular *Activities,* and *Inactivities.* | The power to apply these to the Requirements of the Key, as to *Time* and *Degree.* |

the subsidiary aspects of the
consciously given during the Act of Playing
*lash of consciousness, must nevertheless comprise*

*ENTS* —

---

PHYSICAL attention,—*Outwards* —

| (III) · | (IV) : |
|---|---|
| As to *RESISTANCE,* | As to *PLACE,* in *KEY DESCENT,* |
| *Experienced from each KEY,* | *WHERE each Sound BEGINS* · * |
| ntion and Judgment by means of : the MUSCULAR-SENSE | —Attention and Judgment, by means of : the AURAL-SENSE |

and as to Tone) of each and every note, will be *directly prompted* by our Musical Feeling and Intelligence
and " Aimed"—i e ceased —

Key-movement

ident, when the real problems of Tone-production itself are considered, as they will be, in Parts II and III.

# NOTES TO PART I.

## " ON LISTENING "

Note I —For § 2, Chapter II., page 11. It is so very easy not to "listen" properly ; but instead, merely to *hear*. In the latter case, the only result can be, that we simply hear that which our automatic centres happen to play , whereas, by listening—outwardly and *inwardly*, we shall perhaps succeed in "doing" that which our inner ear directs.

Our eyes can give us a similar difference of experience ; for we may look at a page, a picture, or a scene, and fancy we "see" ; and yet all the while, we are not even trying to perceive A fact we shall immediately discover, if we try to reproduce that page, picture, or scene !

It is the same, if we wish to communicate an idea. Unless we ourselves definitely try to *see* that thought, we shall certainly be unable to communicate it.

We can neither paint, draw, nor write successfully, unless we have an inner picture we wish to fulfil through the implement in our hands.

In fact, a keen—but unconscious—*analysis* of the thing that is to appear, has all the while to precede the "doing." To the extent that such analysis is efficient, to that extent only can the Artist "see" or "feel," as he puts it,— he himself being naturally unaware of his own mental processes. To communicate the thing seen, he must have the power of execution ; he must have the knowledge and experience that will *unconsciously* guide him to choose the exact combinations of colours and shapes, that will render his *Conceptions* —facts of the *Imagination*—into physical *Actuality*.

It is customary to quiz a novice, experimenting with a gun, and to assert, that having aimed most carefully, he after all closes his eyes before pulling the trigger !

It is however no exaggeration to assert that ninety-nine out of every hundred Piano students act analogously at their instrument ! Even if they do go so far as to think of the actual key they mean to deal with, yet, when it comes to the act of depressing it—the very process itself of *using* it to excite sound, then they end, after all, by making an un-*Aimed* muscular effort,—*with their Ears perfectly shut*, so far as attention is concerned ! In playing, *it is the propulsion of the key during its short descent, that has to be "aimed"* ; merely to reach the right key, and to get it down "somehow," does not constitute a musically-directed sound

The mistake arises, from not perceiving that each musical sound must be as much the outcome of the musical Will, as must be the lines constituting a drawing, or piece of penmanship. Non-perception of the fact that a *Sound* is a mere unit, meaningless by itself, arises from the fact, that a musical sound is a so much rarer experience for the majority of individuals, than is the experience of impressions caused by light,—shapeliness being conveyed to us through our eyes all day long.

It is owing to such comparative rarity in the experience of musical-sounds, that something seems actually accomplished when a Piano-key has been made to deliver some sort of sound—no matter how bad, nor how inappropriate !

A mere sound nevertheless no more constitutes musical-sense, than does a mere line constitute a picture when presented to the eye

The moral hence is · that Sound-making only rises above mere tone-*scribbling* when we insist on guiding the requisite Units into a vivid musical-Drawing

### " ON RHYTHM "

NOTE II — For § 5, Chapter II , page 13    There are three distinct ways in which we can pre-determine a single sound    Three distinct forms of Practice result from this fact

*I.* At a sufficiently slow rate of movement, we can give *conscious* attention to each note beforehand , consciously determining not only its Moment and Tone, but also consciously determining *how* it shall individually be obtained from the instrument    Such careful manipulation, demanding as it does a distinct thought *before* each note, requires considerable time    It is the only way to learn new habits of tone-production.    Hence arises the conviction forced upon most players, sooner or later : the need for really SLOW PRACTICE

*II :* We can, at a quicker *tempo*, still consciously will the Time and Tone for each individual sound , although we shall be unable at that speed to pre-realise the means of tone-production involved for each individual sound.    Tone-production must obviously in this case be forthcoming as a previously-formed habit , Habit in this case stimulated into activity by the mere wish or direction for a particular sound-kind.

*III ·* The speed may however be so great as to preclude our directing even the Time of each individual note by a conscious act of volition    The necessary "willing" has then to be relegated to a faculty we possess, that of *semi-automatically* Timing the inside components of note-groups

It is a faculty of the ear and muscles, analogous to the one we use through the eye, which enables us at a glance to discern the exact number contained in a small group of objects, without our actually "counting them up." [1]    We thus discriminate between the various sets of leger lines , the lines that constitute the difference between semi-quavers and demi-semi-quavers , and the sets of lines that form the staves.

We can in fact at great speed, only " will " whole sets of notes    The notes and figures that belong to the Beats being known, the latter are kept in view, and the passage is thus steered along by their means    The inner notes of each beat are in this case merely felt as subdivisions of time *leading up* to each imminent Time-pulse.    For instance, at great speed, groups of four semi-quavers, must be felt as three segmental points of *Crotchet-Division, leading up to* the beginning of the next Crotchet, or Pulse.

This learning to *direct* the minute subdivisions of Time by means of this semi-automatic or unconscious faculty, forms a very important detail in a Performer's Education.

Camille Stamaty, one of the teachers of Liszt, constructed a whole school of Technics—much superior to "Plaidy"—keeping this necessity in view; the suggestive title of the work being : " Le Rhythme des doigts "

---

[1] It is said there have been show men who have trained this faculty to the extent of being able to distinguish at a glance the exact number of balls thrown down, up to about thirty !

## " *PIANO-TALENT*"

Note IV —For §§ 3 and 5, Chapter V , pages 32 and 34   Here once again, is a point where natural endowment differs widely.  Those who, without effort, unconsciously give Attention with full purpose, possess indeed "talent" in the most important respect of all —

For talent itself, in its most general sense—that exhibition of a *strong bias* toward some particular pursuit, may be defined, from its results, as simply : *ability to learn with ease*

Now our ability to learn anything, directly depends on the power of our *Memory*—its impressionability, and its retentiveness , and memorizing again directly depends on the degree of Attention we can provide   Hence, it is, that Power of Attention, or ability to acquire this, is synonymous with : good memory, ease in learning, and in a word "Talent "

A few words of Summary, may prevent misapprehension with regard to the question of Pianoforte "talent "—

Special phases of endowment are needed in addition to general Musicality. These are : a good "piano-voice"—the possession of a sufficiently ample muscular endowment, combined with Ease in mental-muscular discrimination ; a good "Ear," not only for Time, but also particularly for the discernment of subtle distinctions in tone-quantity, and above all, in tone-*Quality ;* "Brains" to enable Attention to be given, combined with a personal bias toward giving the particular form of Attention demanded in playing.

These particular endowments are nevertheless not very far-reaching, unless there be besides, a general endowment musically.  Musical imaginativeness is required, both emotionally and intellectually.  Without that, nothing vivid can be done, however excellent the other, the special, phases of Talent

Moreover, even such endowments do not constitute a player.  To succeed as an Artist, we need besides all that, PERSISTENCE.  That depends on character, on our real love for the Art, and whether we possess Health sound enough to stand the necessary close application

For eventually, as Rubinstein once said to us Royal Academy Students : "real *Hard Work* is the only road to success."

## "*AS TO SELF-CONSCIOUSNESS AND NERVOUSNESS*"

Note V.—For § 7, Chapter V., page 36.  This dread horror kills many a possible player.  Perhaps the following advice may help to eradicate the nervousness resulting from self-consciousness.  Try to realise, that when your audience is really listening, that at that moment they cannot really be conscious of you at all ; for their attention is then given to Music alone, just as yours should be.

Even if a thousand people are looking at the same spot that you are looking at, that fact will not render you self-conscious, nor "nervous."  No, even if they are shouting at the same object that you are shouting at, nor will that do so.  Hence, in performing, try to realise, that the audience is not listening to you, but is listening to the same Music that you are listening *for ; i e.:* that Observation is being directed to the same spot, by yourself and your audience.

It is your duty to "look," with your ears, *at* a certain spot in Music at a definite time ; realise that your listener is looking at that same musical-spot, and that moment you cease being aware that he is listening to *You.* personally.

Moreover, once you feel that that listener's attention is directed to the same musical *Point* that yours is, it will intensify your attention to it, and you will see the music more vividly than in the practise-room !

It is impossible for the listener to concern himself with *you* personally, if he is listening to the sounds provided by your fingers in obedience to your musical wish ; and vice versa : if the listener is aware of you, then he cannot at that moment be aware of the music provided, and the performance cannot then be under criticism. Hence, in either case, there is nothing to be self-conscious about !

In a word, force yourself to realise that the listener is watching for that which you also are trying to hear, and all self-consciousness with its consequent nervousness inevitably vanishes at that moment

Incapacitating nervousness during performance is therefore usually only the result of sheer inattention.

The causes of such inadequate attention are various

They may prove at once remediable by a better understanding, and a consequent better practice, of that which constitutes Performer's Attention

Inadequacy and Uncertainty of Technique (i e , of *Tone-production* itself) does however form perhaps the most potent factor in causing our attention to be distracted from where it should be.

# EXTRACT.

## PART II.

### KEY-TREATMENT

FROM ITS

INSTRUMENTAL ASPECT.

# THE INSTRUMENT.

## (CHAPTER VIII.)

### RECAPITULATORY.

1) : The outer case of the instrument contains *two* distinct portions ; the Instrument-proper, and the Implement by which to excite it into sound.

2) : The instrument-proper consists of : *a)*, the Sounding-board, and *b)*, the Strings, with the wooden or iron Frame to take their tension.

3) : The exciting-implement consists of the " Action " or Mechanism.

4) : This Action, or Mechanism, comprises the Key and all its appurtenances ; these include :—

*a) :* A Leverage-system, see-saw like, designed to facilitate the attainment of a high degree of velocity at the Hammer-end, and thus to communicate Energy to the String in the Form of Motion.

*b) :* The Escapement, a device to enable the hammer to re-bound with and from the string, while the key remains de-pressed.

*c)* · A supplementary device, to enable Repetition to be easily effected.

*d)* . A "check," to catch the hammer on its rebound from the string, so as to prevent its re-striking the string by a further rebound.

5) : The "action" has the following accessories :—

*aa) :* The Damper, to stop the string's vibrations when the key is allowed to rise.

*bb) :* The damper Pedal, to raise the whole of the dampers off the strings, and thus leave them free to vibrate.

*cc) :* The soft pedal, the UNA CORDA pedal.

D

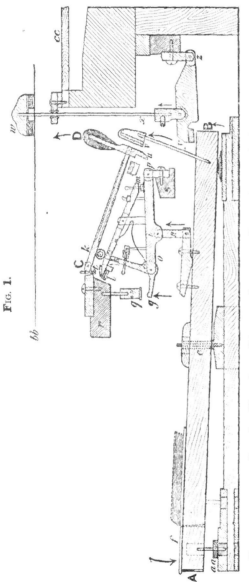

FIG. 1.

DESCRIPTION OF FIG. 1.— The above Diagram forms an illustration of the best type of present-day "Grand-action"; it is a type now adopted as to its principles by all the great makers, although each has slight modifications as to details. It is from a tracing for which I am indebted to the great kindness of Messrs. C. BECHSTEIN.

We, as Pianists, should regard the whole of the mechanism from *A* to *D*, inclusive, as "KEY." The Piano-mechanic however often technically applies this term merely to the wooden rocker *A—B*. This rocker is pivoted at *e* and carries a finger-*plate* of ivory or ebony at *f*.

*C—D* is the "hammer" pivoted at *C*; it has a leather-covered "roller" attached to its underside at *k*. *r* and *s* are *immovable* planks reaching across the full width of the key-board.

The compound ESCAPEMENT is formed by the two straight levers *p—o*, and *l—m*, and by the bent lever or L-crank $g$—$h$ (termed the "hopper") in conjunction with the before-mentioned "roller" attached to the hammer, and the adjustable set-off screws $q$ and $t$.

The operation of the escapement is as follows:—

So long as the key remains unmoved, the Hammer rests, supported through its Roller $k$, upon the end $h$ of the hopper; this latter being for this purpose passed *through* an aperture in the lever $l$—$m$, the "escapement-lever."

When the key is depressed, the whole of the levers concerned in the escapement are raised through the Upright $n$, and through them, the hopper-supported hammer.

Both the end $C$ of the hammer, and the point $p$ of the lever $o$—$p$ however remain stationary, owing to their being pivoted to the planks $r$ and $s$.

To prevent the hammer, on reaching the string, from "blocking" against it, the set-off nut $q$ is so adjusted as to cause the hopper to tilt its $g$-end against this nut at the right moment. As the levers continue to rise while $g$ is arrested by $q$, it follows that $h$ slides from under the Hammer-roller, and as the rise of $l$ has also been meanwhile arrested by the screw $t$, the hammer is thus left free to fall back. It cannot however, fall far away from the string, so long as the key is kept fully depressed, owing to its now resting on the lever $l$—$m$.

It is the latter lever that will enable us now to repeat the note without a full ascent of the finger-end of the key being previously required. For if the key is allowed to rise even slightly, then $h$ will at once slightly descend, as will also the $m$ end of the escapement-lever $l$—$m$; but as $l$ is under a slight pressure from the spring underneath, it continues, for awhile pressing *upward* against its screw $t$ and thus holds the hammer still raised, though not in actual contact with the string. Meanwhile, a moment will however soon be reached, when the Hopper (actuated by the same spring that also gives life to the escapement-lever) will again be able to slip into position under the hammer-roller. We shall thus be able to repeat the note at will. The neat way in which the escapement-lever ($l$—$m$) thus as it were *lifts* and replaces the hammer upon the top of the hopper is a real marvel of mechanical ingenuity.

$v$ is the Check; the $u$ end of the hammer is caught by this on its recoil from the string.

$w$ is the damper, lying on its string; and $y$—$z$ is a little crank by which this is lifted through its wire $x$ by the end of the rocker $A B$ when the key is depressed.

At $aa$ we also see the felt pads that prevent the key being taken down too far—the "key-beds" as they are here termed.

$bb$ represents the position of the string.

$cc$, the edge of the sounding-board.

The arrows indicate the direction of the movements resulting from key-depression.

# ON SOUND.

## (CHAPTER IX )

### RECAPITULATORY.

*a*) : A musical-sound (or note) consists of a series of concussions, equally timed and of equal strength, recurring at a sufficiently great speed to render it impossible for us to recognise the separate impacts delivered upon our ear, which consequently blurs them into a continuous sense-effect.

*b*) · Pitch, is the term used to designate the difference between a high and a low speed in the repetitions of the ear-impacts,— forming the difference between a high and low sound.

*c*) : The pitch of a note depends solely upon the *frequency* with which the air is disturbed or beaten in a given time.

*d*) . The Amount of Tone depends on the Intensity of such disturbance.

*e*) : Most notes are built up of a fundamental strong series of ear-impacts, accompanied by divers quicker and weaker impacts, termed Harmonics.

*f*) : Divergence in the Character, Timbre, or Quality of the tone, arises from the difference in the combination and strength of the harmonics heard with the fundamental sound.

# THE STRING AND ITS BEHAVIOUR.

### (CHAPTER X.)

### RECAPITULATORY.

*a) :* At the Pianoforte, the requisite concussions that form sound are communicated to the atmosphere by means of to-and-fro motions (vibrations) of the String, enhanced by the Sounding-board.

*b) :* The greater the *number* of such vibrations completed by the String per second, the *higher* (more acute in Pitch) is the resulting note.

*c) :* The greater the *extent* of these String vibrations, the *louder* is the note.

*d) :* The string must therefore traverse space more *quickly* the louder the note; since the time available (in which to traverse the larger distance embraced by the more ample vibration) remains the same as for a softer note.

*e) :* To produce much tone, we must therefore induce *much movement* in the string. For the more quickly the string is made to move, the greater will be the distance it can traverse during the course of each complete vibration.   [*Vide* Fig. 2.]

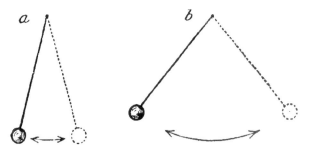

FIG. 2.—Comparison of large with small oscillations of a pendulum; both taking same space of Time for their completion.

*f) :* The string is set into motion by the felt-covered end of the Pianoforte mechanism—the hammer.

*g)* The hammer, upon being brought into contact with the string, *shares* its speed with the latter whilst deflecting it. Both thereupon rebound ; and the hammer, falling away from the string, leaves the latter free to continue in vibration, gradually expending the energy communicated to it, unless stopped by the Damper.[1]

*h) :* The hammer can therefore only communicate movement to the string during the latter's *first* vibration ; and can only do so, during the first *quarter* of such first to-and-fro movement of the string.

*i) ·* As the hammer *ceases to influence* the string the very moment that *Sound begins,* it follows, that this moment *forms the conclusion and cessation* of the Act of Tone-production ; for the string cannot move quicker than it does at that moment, since it has ceased to be under the influence either of Key or Finger.

*j) :* Tone-production at the Pianoforte is therefore a *discontinuous* Act ; an act separate for each note ; and one that *ceases* with the moment when Silence changes into Sound.

*k) ·* Beauty in the Quality of a sound, depends on the string's vibrations tending rather toward the *simple* types of movement than toward the *compound* forms ;—the resulting tone is thus less embarrassed with the harsher harmonics.

*l) :* This simplicity in the string's vibration that furthers beauty of tone (vibration of the string rather as a whole than in sections) depends on the *manner* in which movement is communicated to it.

*m) :* The *harsher* effects arise, when the string is *suddenly* set in motion ; whereas the more *sympathetic* effects arise only when the string is set in motion as *gradually* as possible,

[1] We see therefore, that to obtain a *legato* effect by means of the Pedal, we must let the pedal *rise* as we depress the keys forming the next chord , both the depression of the key and the ascent of the pedal being completed at the same moment     Since the dampers cannot reach their strings until the Pedal is nearly quite up, and as the dampers also act in the same way in connection with the rising key, it also follows that it becomes an inexorable rule in *legato* playing, *not to depress the pedal at the same moment as a key* the sound of which we wish to sustain, but instead to do so immediately *after* the completion of the descent of such key.     Correct Pedalling during Legato  the putting down of the Pedal, thus forms a close *syncopation* following the    in time of the notes.

# THE KEY.

## (CHAPTER XI.)

### RECAPITULATORY.

*a):* We find that the Key is a Speed-tool ; and that the laws that govern the use of other speed-tools must therefore equally apply in the case of the Pianoforte key.

*b):* We should always bear in mind, as previously suggested, that this Tool is akin to the *See-Saw* in principle.[1]

*c):* This will prevent our being tempted either to *squeeze* it upon the pads beneath, or to *punch* its surface viciously, in our efforts to make Tone by its means.

*d):* We shall then, on the contrary, take hold of it—*upon* it, and realising its resistance, feel it to be so intimately in connection with our finger-tip, as to seem literally a *continuation* of it.

*e):* Projecting our minds meanwhile to the opposite end of this tool—the hammer-end, we shall bring Force in the shape of Weight and Muscular-exertion to bear upon its *handle*—its ivory or ebony end.

*f):* We shall so *time* the application of this force, both as regards Amount and Gradation, that we shall ensure that the desired

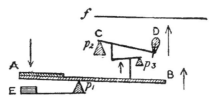

FIG. 3.—Diagrammatic representation of the *principle* of the compound-leverage involved, with omission of all details of the mechanism.

A—B wooden rocker, with finger plate at A. C—D hammer. *f* string. E keypad. *p*1, *p*2, *p*3, are immovable centres or pivots.

---

[1] It is well to keep this simile in mind, since it is so manifestly futile to continue pressing down one end of a See-Saw, after this has reached the ground, if our purpose be to induce movement at its other end. (*Vide also Chapter VIII., and above Fig. 3.*)

speed of the Key—and String—is reached before our end of the tool is brought into contact with its underlying pad, and we shall thus have succeeded in obtaining the exact tone-shading which our musical conscience prompted us to desire. [*Vide* Figs. 3 and 4.]

Fig. 4.—The difference between "sudden" and "gradual" key-depression.

*g): * Of the two horizontally converging thick lines in Fig. 4 (both the above diagrams), the *upper* line (*aa*) illustrates the position of our end of the key when at rest—at "surface-level"; while the lower of these lines represents the position of the key's surface when fully depressed.

The vertical (dotted) lines in both diagrams are meant to exhibit the *degree* in the key's motion *during descent,* respectively in brilliant and in sympathetic tone-production.

In diagram *A,* we have Energy applied *suddenly*—"avec attaque." Here the dotted lines *c* (supposed to represent the *degree* of speed) are seen to start at once *some distance* apart, but they remain *only thus far apart* to the end of the key's descent; for the key-descent is so *sudden* that it is practically impossible to attain any *increase* in speed during it.

In diagram *B,* the key has on the contrary been reached practically without percussion, without suddenness,—"sans attaque." The dotted lines *d* therefore here commence together, and they *widen out* to represent the Speed-*crescendo* that can now be induced during descent; for the key is in this case started on its journey almost imperceptibly, but has energy applied to it in *increasing ratio* during its short-lived descent, thus giving that almost unpercussive attack *of the string* whence arises Beauty of tone.[1]

[1] It seems well-nigh incredible that we should thus be able to GRADE the motion of a key (as demanded for sympathetic tone) during the minute interval of time expended during key-descent. Many of the muscular acts of our

every-day existence are however found to be equally minutely graded, when we analyse them.

It is even possible (although extremely difficult) directly to grade key descent in this requisite manner by an exertion of the Will. This is however happily unnecessary, otherwise our Technique would for ever remain cumbrous and uncertain, for we can, by supplying the requisite MUSCULAR CONDITIONS, encompass this end in quite a simple and reliable way, and it is thus that the effect of sympathetic-tone is wrought in actuality.          By in fact placing the various muscles belonging to the Finger, Hand and Arm in the requisite relationship to each portion of the limb and the key, we are able to apply energy through so elastic a medium, that the desired gradation during key-descent accomplishes itself almost automatically, and with corresponding certainty.

To enable us to provide these requisite muscular conditions, we must study key-treatment from its *Muscular Aspect* This aspect of the study of Touch is dealt with in Part III. and the Parts that follow it.

# RECAPITULATORY AND SUMMARY

OF THE MAIN CONCLUSIONS OF

## PART II

*a)*: The Pianoforte Key is a machine to facilitate the production of Speed in the String. It is a compound-lever, akin in principle to the See-saw.

*b)*: It follows, that Tone-production can only be effected by giving Motion to the Key; since this forms our only means of conveying motion to the String.

*c)*: Energy brought to bear upon the Key *ceases* to create Tone, the moment that the place in key-descent is reached, where the hammer's motion culminates, and causes Sound to *begin*.

*d)*: The act itself of Tone-production can hence never take longer than it does in the most extreme *Staccatissimo*.

*e)*: The Ear apprises us of this moment more quickly than can any other of our senses ; hence we must *listen* for the beginning of sound, if we would have Accuracy in tone-production.

*f)* · The greater the total speed we induce during each individual key-descent, the greater is the Tone-*quantity*.

*g)* · The more *gradually* this key-speed is attained, the more beautiful is the Tone-*character*,—the fuller, more "sympathetic," singing and carrying is its *quality*.

*h)*: The more *sudden* the key-depression, the harsher is the resulting Tone-quality ; it may be more "brilliant," but it will be less effective in carrying power.

*i)*: The *softest* possible sound is obtained, when *Weight* is brought upon the key until a point is reached where the key's opposition (or resistance) to movement is just overcome—and it consequently slips down with the most gentle movement compatible with its hammer reaching the string.

*j)*: Such amount of Weight, allowed to remain resting upon

the key, *beyond* the moment that the latter's full depression is reached, forms the effect of TENUTO. The duration of such Tenuto is determined by the duration of such Resting.

*k)*. The effect of LEGATO is induced by *transferring* such continuously resting light Weight from key to key ; such Transference being unbroken for each Musical Phrase.

• *l):* Weight of less amount than this, *insufficient* therefore to cause key-depression, may be left resting on the keys without causing either Tenuto or Legato.

It is such *lightness* in resting, that forms the Basis of all STACCATO effects, provided it is combined with an accurately-aimed Promptness in the *cessation* of the Energy that causes key-*descent ;* for the keys are in this case left free to *rebound* the moment that Tone-production is completed.

*m)*. Such combination (of light Resting and accurate Ceasing of the act of key-depression) also forms the secret of all great Agility in playing.

*n):* It is futile to *squeeze* the key upon its bed with the object of inducing Tone ; since sound, if produced at all, is given off *before* the key reaches its full depression.

*o):* It is almost as futile to attempt to obtain good tone by *knocking* the key ; since the concussion here caused at the key-surface forms *waste* of the Energy intended to create tone, and thus engenders *inaccuracy* in the tonal-result,—the actual tone obtained not corresponding to the tone intended.

*p)* · We find (also vide Part III) that instead of squeezing the key-bed, or hitting the key-top, that correct Tone-production demands:—that the finger be brought comparatively gently into contact with the key-board surface, so that the Energy requisite to move the key may be there estimated by our *sense of key-resistance*. As the key-resistance varies with each change in Tone-shading, this will lead to the requisite *muscular-conditions* being almost automatically prompted into existence,—in accurate response therefore to the dictates of our musical-consciousness as to **Time, Tone-amount, Tone-quality, and Duration.**

# EXTRACT.

## PART III.

### KEY-TREATMENT

FROM ITS

### MUSCULAR ASPECT.

# PART III.

KEY-TREATMENT FROM ITS MUSCULAR ASPECT.

THE LINK BETWEEN KEY AND MUSCLE—OUR SENSE OF
KEY-RESISTANCE.

(CHAPTER XIII)

## RECAPITULATORY.

*a)*: Part II. demonstrates that each and every sound-colour—
both of quality and quantity—depends on the way we *move* the
key during each short-lived process of descent.

*b)* · The requirements the key exhibits, differ therefore with
each difference in sound-kind—sound-shading or inflection.

*c)*: It follows that we must precisely adjust our efforts to
meet these constantly varying requirements.

*d)*: Our only means of judging what these are, is through
watching the Resistance the key itself offers us, before and during each descent,—the " giving-way point " of the key.

*e)*: It is only by employing our *" Resistance-sense"* (the Muscular-sense and its co-operatives) that we can be apprised with
certainty of these inexorable requirements of the key.

*f)*: This sense hence forms the *Link* between the key-board
and ourselves.

*g)*: It is not enough to use merely the sense of Contact or
Touch, we must insist on feeling the actual *resistance* the key
offers to our muscles before and during descent.

*h)*: So intimate will the connection thus formed be, that
finger and key will appear as one to us ;—the whole leverage-
system, from shoulder to hammer-end, will seem as one living
lever to us.

*i) :* Certainty, both as to Notes and as to Expression, can alone be secured in this way.

*j) :* In slow successions of notes, each one is to be thus individually felt and judged.   In quick passages, the separate units are merged into one general sensation and judgment of the keyboard.

*k) :* Attention to key-resistance also compels *Musical-attention :* for we cannot muscularly *judge* the key as to Tone and Time, unless we have a sound in our mind, exactly dictated by our Musical-feeling at that moment.

## ON KEY-CONTACT.

### (CHAPTER XIV.)

### RECAPITULATORY.

*a) :* The finger-tip must reach the key with but little percussion.

*b) :* The preliminary *fall* of the limb upon the key-surface, should be free from perceptible exertion ; it should arise rather from Relaxation.

*c) :* It is not until we reach the key, that we can *commence* the act of *pressing it into motion,*—the act proper of tone-production.

*d) :* The act of reaching the key, and the act of setting it into motion, need not necessarily be separate ; the two may coalesce into an unbroken descent.

*e) :* Contact, may, on the other hand, be made some time before the note is required ; several notes at a time may thus be previously felt, in certain rapid runs.

*f) :* The difference between Sudden and Gradual depression of the key should mostly depend on the *condition* of the muscles during the subsequent operation.[1]

*g) :* Harsh sounds do not carry ; hence they do not sound so full and "grand" a little way off, as they seem to do close to the instrument.

---

[1] That is, it should depend upon what we do *during* the operation of tilting the Key into sound.

*h)*: Contact, and subsequent key-treatment, must be modified according to the softness or hardness of the hammer; a soft hammer requires more "driving" for the brilliant effects, while a harder hammer requires greater *elasticity* in the limb itself for the sympathetic effects.

*i)*: Every key *should be reached* from as great a distance as conveniently possible; this so, that the movement towards (and with the key) may be *as free as possible;* and so that we can the better *individualise* each finger in the quicker passages.

*j)*: Amplitude in preparatory movement must not be insisted upon in very rapid passages, as it may lead to stiffening, and worse—even muscular damage.

*k)*: Proper Contact with the key, is the first step towards Accuracy in Expression.

Σ

(CHAPTER XV.)

## RECAPITULATORY, AND DEFINITIONS.

*a)* : Touch consists of two concepts, and acts :

(*a*) a " Resting," (*b*) an " Added-impetus."

*b)* : The act of Resting is analogous to that of *breath-control* in Speech, and Song. Phrasing is mainly made evident through the continuance or discontinuance of this element of Resting, or its equivalent.

*c)* : The act of Resting is *continuous* during each phrase in all finger-passages, whether these be Legato or Staccato. It is also in a sense continuous even during " wrist " and arm passages.

*d)* : We may " rest " upon the key-board in two distinct ways :—

(1) We may do so with weight no greater than the keys will bear *without* their being thereby depressed. In this form it is the Basis of *staccato*.

(2) We may do so, with slightly more weight, sufficient just to *overbalance* the key into descent, and thus to provoke its softest sound. This forms the basis of all Tenuti and Legati.

In the first case we rest at the *surface-level* of the key-board ; in the second case we rest at the *depressed-level* of the key-board.

*e)* : The non-percussive renewal of Contact with the key-board forms an equivalent to the first-named form of the Resting.

*f)* : The *first*, or lighter form of the Resting (at the surface-level of the key-board) keeps us informed *where* the key is in space, and of the degree of resistance it offers to movement ; so that we may know *whence* to commence the stresses needed for tone-production, and their required intensity.

Such Resting, unaided, is incapable of creating tone ; the Added-impetus is therefore here required in any case to form the tone.

*g)* : The *second*, or heavier form of Resting (at depressed key-level) includes the first. It compels the fingers to retain their keys in a depressed condition, as required for Legato and Tenuto, and it gives us besides the same information as does the Surface-resting.

*h)* : This *second* form of Resting should outbalance the key with no more weight than will just suffice to overcome the friction and inertia of the Key and String. This Resting, unaided, is competent to produce soft sounds ; and it forms the sole means of obtaining the true, absolute *pp*.

But when *greater tone-amounts* than *pp* are desired, an Added-impetus is also here required, just as in the Staccato form of the Resting.[1]

*i)* : Such " weighed " *pp*, moreover forms the only *simple* form of Touch ; since it consists of but one act—that of Resting.

*j)* : All other forms of touch are *compound*, for these require the co-operation of the Added-impetus with the Resting.

*k)* : The muscular-difference between Staccato and Tenuto consists therefore in the *difference of level* at which the Resting is accomplished. Such difference in level depends upon the slight difference in the Weight continuously resting upon the key-board. The heavier form of the Resting compels the fingers to continue working against their keys, *beyond* the completion of each individual act of tone-production; while the lighter form permits them to rebound with the key.

*l)* : Legato consists of a sequence of *complete* Tenuti. The Resting is here transferred from finger to finger ;—the transference being in this case effected from the bottom of a depressed key, to the *surface* of the key whose deflection we intend to start ; whereas in Staccato, the transference is effected entirely at the surface-level of the key-board.

*m)* : As all forms of Staccato, Tenuto and Legato (except absolute *pp*) require the Added-impetus to form the tone, we must be careful that Energy, thus applied for tone-production, is promptly and completely *ceased* when sound is reached.

[1] It is permissible to induce *slight* increments of tone beyond *pp* by means of slight increases in the transferred or " passed-on " Resting-weight. This for instance is appropriate in many of the gentle, but swiftly swirling arabesques or *cadenzi* of Chopin and Liszt.

*n) :* Both Tone-quantity and quality (except *ppp*) depend on the form and application of this Added-impetus. It is the source of all colouring.

*o) :* Touch consists therefore of a *continuous* Element (the Resting) which determines Duration ; interspersed with a *discontinuous* Element (the Added-impetus) which determines Sound-kind.[1]

*p) :* In playing, we must hence be careful (*a*) to select the *right* kind of Resting, and to see that this is *real ;* and (*b*) that the Added-impetus is accurately " aimed " to culminate and cease with each sound-beginning, and that it is muscularly of the required kind.

---

[1] A Synopsis follows in tabular form.

# TABLE

## TOUCH
Consists of:—

| THE RESTING<br>The continuous Element | THE ADDED-IMPETUS<br>The dis-continuous Element |
|---|---|
| Is coexistent with the duration of each phrase or sustained note: Either absolutely continuous, as in all finger passages, or of *resumed* continuance, in Hand and Arm passages. | Lasts only during the moment of key-deflection, and ceases instantly with the emission of sound, no matter what the kind of tone. |
| **FIRST, OR LIGHTER FORM,** at key-surface only, is<br>**The Basis of all Staccati.**<br>Not heavy enough to depress the key; hence permits the key to rebound on the conclusion of the act of key-depression. | Required to produce the sound in all *staccati*; also in all Tenuti and Legati *of greater* Tone-amount than pp. |
| **SECOND, OR HEAVIER FORM,** at key-bed; includes the first form, and is<br>**The Basis of all Tenuti and Legati.**<br>Suffices to depress the key *at its softest*, and to retain it depressed.*<br><br>*(a)* Tenuto, and all degrees of Duration less than that, down to staccato.<br>*(b)* Legato, when the Tenuti are transferred from finger to finger. | Its many-sidedness permits all tone-differences both of Quality and Quantity. The various forms consequently required of it, are described in the Chapters that follow. |

* The Resting and the Added impetus are hence identical in ppp-Tenuto or Legato, which thus forms the only simple form of Touch.

(CHAPTER XVI.)

## RECAPITULATORY.

*a)* : The limb employed in playing consists of four main portions, four levers:—the Finger, the Hand, the Fore-arm and the
Upper-arm.

*b)* : Each portion or segment is individually provided with
muscles ; we can therefore control each portion separately—both
as to exertion, and as to lapse of it.

*c)* : The finger can be exerted in two completely different
ways ;—the Bent or *Thrusting* attitude ; and the Flat, or *Clinging*
attitude.[1]

*d)* : Exertion implies muscular-action. For every exertion
we are able to make in any direction, we are also provided with
muscles to provide the *reverse* exertion.

*e)* : Exertion of a muscle leads to a visible result—motion of
the limb-section to which it is attached, only when there be
nothing to prevent such motion.

*f )* : Four quite distinct effects may hence result from a muscular-exertion :—

> (1) It may lead to an actual *movement* of the portion of
> the limb to which it is attached ;
>
> (2) It may cause that limb-section to *bear* against some
> outside object,—such as the Pianoforte key ;
>
> (3) Or may cause it to bear against another portion of
> the *same* limb ;
>
> (4) Lastly, if allowed to act in sympathy with its
> *opposite* neighbour, it will deter that muscle (or set) in its
> work; thus leading to the work being done un-freely, or
> even inducing for the time a total stiffening or rigidity of
> the involved portion of the limb.

*g)* : The isolation of each set of muscular impulses from its
opposite set, is hence the first and most important step towards
acquiring a correct Technique ; since any inexpertness in this

[1] *Vide* Figs 6 and 7, next page.

respect causes a "stiffness" of Finger and Wrist, etc., that in-fallibly precludes accuracy either in tonal or in rhythmical result.

*b) :* RELAXATION—Ease, derived from the omission of all un-necessary muscular-exertion (in conjunction with accuracy in its application to the key), forms the main secret of all *easy* and therefore accurate Playing.

THE DIFFERENCE BETWEEN THRUSTING AND CLINGING FINGER:

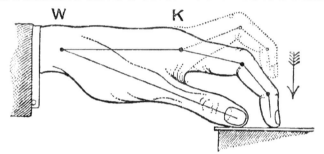

Fig. 6.—The Thrusting (Bent) Finger-attitude.

The position is with depressed key; the dotted lines exhibit the index-finger fully raised.
W is the Wrist, K the Knuckle.

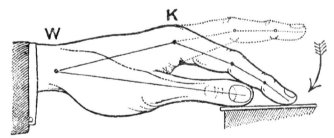

Fig. 7.—The Clinging (Flat) Finger-attitude.

The position is with depressed key; the dotted lines exhibit the index-finger fully raised.

The above two figures are designed to exhibit the two opposite Finger-attitudes employed in playing. They consist of differences in movement and action, and they demand totally opposite *conditions* (states) of the Upper-arm.

The actual *Position* assumed by the Wrist-joint and Knuckle may vary rather considerably, without interfering with the due operation of these two opposite sets of Muscular-conditions :—

The main point with the Thrusting-attitude, Fig. 6, is, that the Knuckle must be sufficiently high to allow it easily to take the *thrust* of the fingers,— wherefore some teachers bend the fingers very fully and hold the Knuckle exceedingly high with a low-dropped wrist.

The Clinging-action (Fig 7) even admits of the Wrist-joint being either held quite high, or of being dropped below the level of the key-board,—provided no running passage be attempted in the latter case.   It also admits of the finger being as much curved with full key-depression as in thrusting-action— but such contracted position in this case modifies the tone-character from that resulting from the fully "flat,"—and "elastic" finger

The main difference to be noted by the eye, is, that when the finger is *well-raised* as a preliminary, it is much curved in the first attitude, whereas it is al most fully opened out in the second.

THE REQUIRED ACTIONS AND INACTIONS.

(CHAPTER XVII )

## RECAPITULATORY.

*a)* : The Act of Touch implies levering weight upon the key, to cause its deflection.

*b)* : This leverage-power is obtained :

1) by exerting the Finger,

2) by exerting the Hand in conjunction with the Finger.

*c)* : When the finger is exerted against the key, it bears upwards by recoil against the Knuckle of the hand, and with equal force.

*d)* : The hand, when it is exerted, bears downwards upon the finger at the knuckle, and it likewise bears upwards (by reaction) with equal force—against the Arm at the Wrist-joint.

*e)* : At the Wrist-joint, these two combined forces meet the weight of the Arm ; and it is therefore the Arm that forms the Basis for the operation of the finger and hand against the key.

*f)* : The arm may be employed for this purpose in two distinct ways :

1) It may be *self-supported* by its muscles.

2) It may be left *un-supported* during the action of tone-production.

*g)* : Arm-weight, if insufficient for extreme *fortes*, may be supplemented by a bearing-up against the Shoulder. The weight of the Shoulder and even of the Body itself thus forms the ultimate Basis, or Foundation. Body-*force* must never be employed instead.

*h)* : All sensation, during the Act of Touch, must invariably be *upwards*.

This is so because all the work done reacts upwards against Weight—thus producing a stepping-up against the Knuckle and the Wrist, and even against the Shoulder in extreme cases.

*i) :* There are therefore *Three Muscular Components* from which we can construct the Act of Touch, viz. ·

1) Finger-exertion,
2) Hand-exertion,
3) Arm-weight, and its co-operatives.

*j) :* These three components divide, broadly, into two distinct kinds—Exertion and Weight.    The two opposite *elements* thus recognised, meet at the Wrist-joint.    Exertion, there bearing upwards, meets the downward tendency of Weight.

*k) :* The total *quantity* of tone (loudness) depends on the total amount of Energy used against the key during its descent, and obtained from these two sources.

*l) :* The *quality* of the tone mainly depends on how we *start* this combination of Exertion and Weight against the key, viz. :

1): If we want tone of a beautiful quality, we must start the combination by Weight (*i.e.,* by Arm-release) ; for the key is then more gradually driven into Speed.

2): If we want a tone of a brilliant, aggressive, or sharp quality, we must start the combination by Exertion (of the finger and hand) ; for the key is then driven more suddenly into Speed.

We thus obtain two completely different *genera* of Touch— " Weight-touch " and " Muscular-touch."

*m) :* The Tone-quality is further influenced by which *attitude* we adopt of the Finger and Upper-arm conjointly.    There are two opposite attitudes :

1) The *Clinging*, or *flat*-finger attitude.
2) The *Thrusting*, or *bent*-finger attitude.

The Clinging-attitude makes for beauty of the tone,—the *singing*-quality, with its carrying character : because the whole limb is here in its most *elastic* condition.

The Thrusting-attitude makes for brilliancy and aggressive-ness, with its " short " Tone-character ; because the whole limb is then in a more rigid condition.[1]

[1] *Vide* Figs 6 and 7, also Figs. 8 and 9, pages 63 and 74 of this work.

*n):* To use the Clinging-attitude, we must leave the Upper-arm more or less relaxed during the moment of tone-production; thus causing the Elbow to tend to hang on to the fingers.
Weight thus set free permits the finger to cling to the key to the necessary extent.

The finger, in thus tending to drag the Elbow towards the key-board, should be used *as a whole,*—all three joints nearly straight or "flat."

*o):* To use the Thrusting-attitude, we must on the contrary support the Upper-arm—more or less forwards.           This permits the finger to thrust against the key to the necessary extent, the thrust being taken by the Elbow.

The finger, in thus tending to thrust against the Elbow, is used in a very rounded (or bent) position, and it tends to *un-bend* towards and with the key; the nail-joint remaining almost upright.           The action is like that of the leg in walking up-stairs.

*p):* Most of the work done by the finger, should be derived from the part of the finger next to the knuckle—the knuckle-phalanx, *i.e.:* The part of the finger next to the knuckle (or hand), is the part that should do most of the work.

This applies equally in "flat" and "bent" attitudes.[1]

*q):* The action of the finger, in both attitudes, is best understood at first, by turning the hand palm upwards, and lifting a weight by the tip of the finger.

*r):* If we require the most sympathetic tone, we must combine Clinging-attitude with Weight-initiative.           Remembering that the slightest "putting-down" of the key, will destroy the desired result.

*s):* If we want a sharp incisive tone (sacrificing carrying-power) then we must combine the Thrusting-attitude with Muscular-initiative.

*t):* Finger-touch, Hand-touch ("Wrist-action") and Arm-touch, are terms *not* referring to the action or otherwise of the three various parts designated.           They merely refer to *movements* of those parts, respectively.           Whether an actual *movement* of the

---

[1] *Vide* Fig 11, also Figs 8 and 9, pages 74 and 75 of this work.

Finger, Hand or Arm accompanies key-descent, depends purely upon *which* of the three components provides slightly more Energy. Thus:

1): Finger-touch (or movement) *may* involve the operation of all three of the muscular components—finger-exertion, hand-exertion, and arm-weight. Or, finger and hand exertion may alone be used; or, the finger-exertion alone.

2): Hand-touch (or movement) *must* involve finger-exertion, and *may* also involve arm-weight.

3): Arm-touch (or movement) *must* involve exertion both of the finger and the hand, accompanied by Arm-lapse.

*u)*: Choice of movement is chiefly determined by the actual speed of the passage; *i.e.*: It is the actual speed of the passage that mostly determines which part of the limb we must move :—

1): Arm-movement (or touch) should be employed when the passage is sufficiently slow to admit of it.

A more or less slight raising of the whole limb off the key-board renders the act of phrasing clearer. The first note of a phrase is therefore nearly always played by arm-descent.

2): Hand-movement (or touch) must be chosen, when the notes succeed each other too quickly to be conveniently played by arm-touch.

3): Finger-movement (or touch), as it provides the shortest lever, must be chosen for passages beyond the speed-capacity of Hand-touch.

4): Finger-movement (or touch) is however also employed for slower passages, and even for the slowest. This, because we can only obtain a true Legato through the intervention of the fingers, thus enabling us to transfer the second kind of Resting from key to key.

*v)*: Choice of Touch-*formation* (the Muscular-combination employed during the act of key-depression) is however even more important than choice of Touch-movement.

There are three main forms of such combination ; forming Three Species of Touch-formation or construction :

1) : Finger-exertion alone, with passive Hand and self-supported Arm.

2) : Hand-exertion behind the Finger-exertion, with self-supported Arm.

3) : Arm-weight (etc.) released in conjunction with the Finger-and-hand exertion.[1]

*w)* : The weight of the arm, thus required for the "Added-impetus," is obtained by omitting its self-support for the time.

The *whole* arm must be released from the shoulder (to the necessary extent), not the Fore-arm only.        Movement of the arm, is moreover no guarantee that it is really descending of its own weight.

*x)* : Arm-weight thus employed in the form of "Added-impetus" during the act of tone-production, must cease to bear upon the key the moment sound is reached ; but we must not cause this cessation, by trying to lift the arm off the keys.   On the contrary, the arm must be made to resume its self-support *automatically*. This it will do, if we "leave it in the lurch," at the Wrist, by promptly ceasing all work of the finger and hand against the key, the moment that sound is reached.

*y)* : The continuous weight required to form the second (or slightly heavier) kind of "Resting," upon which depends the effect of Tenuto and Legato, is obtained in the same way : A very slight release of the *whole* arm suffices ; not dis-continuous as for the Added-impetus, but here continuous, and no greater than just sufficient to overbalance the key into descent.

*z)* : This same process also forms the absolute-*pp* Weight-touch.

[1] This all-important matter, the muscular-construction of the act of Touch in its Three main Species, and the Varieties of these, is more fully dealt with in Chapter XIX., which see.

To obtain it, we must be careful really to weigh the key down by such arm-release, and not in the least to *put* it down by mus‐cular-initiative.

*aa) :* True Legato, we found, is only possible in finger-pas‐sages ;[1] for the Tenuto form of the Resting (or *pp* Weight-touch) must here be transferred from finger to finger during the continu‐ance of each phrase.

This transfer should be effected by timing the *previous* finger to cease its weight-supporting activity at the moment that the next key's descent is required to *commence.* Thus the new finger is compelled to take up its duties automatically in response to the weight being " left in the lurch " by the preceding finger.

*bb) :* Without any Added-impetus, this forms *pp* Transfer-touch. Here again we must be careful not directly to influence the new finger's depression ; we must instead insist on the previous finger giving way at the right moment.

*cc) :* The following facts will now be clearer :—

Pianissimo Weight-touch[2] accompanies *all* forms of Tenuto ; —since all tone beyond *pp* must be supplied by one of the multi‐farious forms of the Added-impetus.

Pianissimo Weight-transfer touch, in the same way accom‐panies all Legati of greater tone-amount than *pp*.

Tenuto and Legato of *more* tone than *pp*, hence consist of *pp* Weight-touch or Weight-transfer-touch respectively, with a tone-making operation *added thereto* for each note—the Added-impetus, the latter as short-lived as in Staccatissimo.

*dd) :* For the first (or Staccato) form of the Resting, the weight of the hand alone is sufficient. For this purpose, the hand must lie quite loosely upon the keys. Tone, of whatever kind, must of course be obtained by employment of the Added-impetus in one of its many forms.

*ee) :* Invisible adjustments of the Forearm are constantly re‐quired in a *rotary* or *tilting* direction, to ensure Evenness of effect from all the fingers ; and also to enable the fingers at either side

---

[1] Except by intervention of the Damper-pedal    Chap  XV., etc.
[2] Already considered in Chapter XV.

of the hand to pronounce their notes prominently. These adjustments enable us to support either side of the hand off the keys when required; and enable us also to influence either side with more force or weight when that is required.

*ff)*: This forms *Rotation-touch*, when such adjustments are allowed to become visible as a tilting movement of the hand.

*gg)*: Lateral movements of the Hand and of the Wrist itself are also required to ensure Evenness. Without such movements, it would be impossible to connect without break or jerk the various fingering-positions out of which passages are formed. These side to side movements (whether great or small) must be absolutely unrestrained.

*hh)*: Rotary and lateral freedom of the Wrist enables one to feel always "ready" over every note beforehand.

*ii)*: Purely Vertical freedom of the Wrist-joint itself must be insisted upon, besides this rotary and lateral freedom. Only in this way can a really free Wrist be ensured.

*jj)*: *Per contra*: if we always insist on feeling *ready* and *vertical* over each note, before attempting its production, we shall fulfil these three conditions of freedom of the Wrist—laterally, rotarily, and vertically.

*kk)*: To enable us to reach closely adjacent notes, slight lateral movements of the fingers themselves suffice.

*ll)*: To enable us to take larger skips, but such as do not exceed about two octaves in extent, we must use lateral movements of the Forearm, with the Elbow as the apparent pivot. These are mainly induced by a partial rotation of the Upper-arm.

*mm)*: For still larger skips, the whole arm, from the shoulder, must move sideways. Such large skips however become exceedingly uncertain, if attempted beyond a comparatively slow speed.

*nn)*: Muscular - discriminations in very definite directions have thus been proved requisite. These should be studied in the Table annexed to this chapter.

## TABLE

OF THE MAIN MENTAL-MUSCULAR DISCRIMINATIONS REQUIRED TO
ENABLE US TO FULFIL THE CONDITIONS OF ACTION AND IN-
ACTION EMPLOYED DURING THE ACT OF TOUCH.

I. *Ability independently to leave lax—unsupported by their respective muscles :—*

(a) The *Hand,*  
(b) The *Fore-arm,*  
(c) The *Upper-arm,*  
(d) The *Shoulder,*  

so that we shall be able to set free their Weight as required, independently of any downward exertion of the finger or hand.[1]

II. *Isolation of the Finger's down-activity (or exertion) from that of the Hand*—ability to exert the finger against the key, independently of any *exertion* downwards of the hand.[2]

III. *Isolation of the Hand's down-activity from that of the Arm*—ability to exert the hand downwards behind the fingers upon the keys, even to its fullest extent, without permitting any down-activity of the Arm.[3]

IV. *Freedom of the Finger's action*—isolation of the finger's down-exertion from its opposite exertion—freeing the finger's down-exertion from the upward one.[4]

V *Freedom of the Hand's action*—isolation of the hand's down-exertion from the upward one.[5]

VI. *Discrimination between the Thrusting and the Clinging application of the Finger against the key*—with its correlated alternative, either of *forward-supported* or *lax-left* Elbow and Upper-arm.[6]

VII *Freedom in the rotary-adjustments of the Fore-arm—*

—a) ability to leave the fore-arm *lax* in a tilting direction towards either side of the hand,—both fifth-finger and thumb sides.  
—b) ability to *exert* the fore-arm rotarily in either of these directions.[7]

[1] §§ 2, 3, 4, 6, 7, 22.  
[2] § 6, etc.  
[3] § 6, etc.  
[4] § 23, also last chapter.  
[5] § 23, also last chapter.  
[6] §§ 12-15, also last chapter  
[7] § 31.

These references apply to Chapter XVII of "The Act of Touch."

VIII *Freedom of the Wrist and Hand horizontally*—
—isolation of the muscular act that moves the hand to one side laterally, from the act that moves it in the opposite direction ; required to assist the thumb in turning under, and the fingers in turning over.[1]

IX *Ability accurately to time the cessation of the down-exertion of the Finger, employed during key-descent*—
—ability to "*aim*" this exertion, so that it may culminate and cease at the moment of sound emission[2]

X *Ability accurately to time the cessation of the down-exertion of the Hand, employed during key-descent*—
—ability to *aim* the hand-exertion, so that it may also be directed by the ear, like that of the finger.[3]

XI. *Ability accurately to time the cessation of* WEIGHT, *employed to produce tone*—
—ability to time the application of any Arm-weight employed for the creation of key-descent, so that it may culminate and cease at the moment of sound emission.[4]

XII. *Freedom in the movements required of the Finger, the Hand, the Fore-arm and the Upper-arm in bringing the finger-tips into place over their required notes, antecedent to the act of key-depression*—
—freedom in the lateral, or side-to-side movements : (a) of the Fingers and Thumb, (b) of the Hand, (c) of the Fore-arm, with the elbow as a pivot, and (d) of the Elbow and Upper-arm itself.[5]

[1] § 34
[2] §§ 24 and 28, *vide also " The Added Impetus," last chapter.*
[3] § 24, *vide The Added Impetus, last chapter.*
[4] A cessation that must be caused, by the arm-supporting muscles acting in strict response to the timed *cessation* of the up-bearing action of the finger and hand against the arm at the wrist, during the act of key-depression.*
[5] §§ 24 37 38, and 39.
* § 24 and 1st Chapter.

F

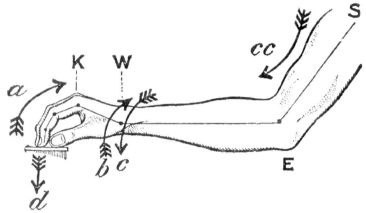

FIG. 8.—DESCRIPTION: * The arrows in the above, represent the directions in which the forces tend during BENT finger-attitude.

*a* and *b* denote the direction of the energy resulting by recoil from the *thrusting* action of the finger and hand against the key, and manifesting itself upwards and backwards respectively at the knuckle and wrist joints.

*c* and *cc*, the energy that balances this, derived from arm-weight and force.

K is the Knuckle; W the Wrist; E the Elbow, and S the Shoulder.

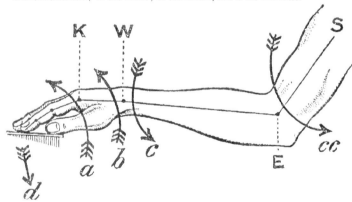

FIG. 9.—DESCRIPTION: The arrows denote the tendencies during FLAT finger-attitude.

*a* and *b* denote the direction of the energy resulting from the finger and hand *clinging* to the key, and how it manifests itself as an upward and forward-drawing stress at the knuckle and wrist.

*c* and *cc*, the direction in which the energy tends, that is set free in this case at the elbow and wrist, and derived from Arm-weight through its release.

*d*, in both Figs., shows the direction of the total Energy-result.—*vertical* upon the key during its descent, and slightly dragging, in Fig. 9.

* In Fig. 6 the Bent-finger was shown with the wrist-position almost as high as it may be; in the above figure, the lower position-limit is illustrated. On this point, the various "Methods" differ completely as to their Dogma. The fact is that the precise position adopted should vary in accordance with variety in hand-conformation. (*Vide Part IV.*, "On Position.")

FIG. 11.—Faulty action of the *two front phalanges* of the finger, showing the result of these being exerted with greater force than the Knuckle-phalanx—which should be the main *working*-lever of the finger.

NOTE:

*The Staccatissimo.*

Besides the *passive* Staccato so far considered,—a Staccato induced and assured (a) by insisting on the continuous Resting-weight being so attenuated as *not* to compel the fingers to continue working beyond the moment that sound is reached, and (b) by insisting on accurately timing the cessation of each finger's action; besides this natural Staccato, there is also a forced kind,—a Staccatissimo, in which the key-bed is as it were "kicked" against by each finger.

While the *raising*-muscles of the finger and hand are not required in the natural Staccato, we find that in this "kick-off" Staccato they do come into operation in a slight measure. But even here, they must under no circumstances be directly *willed* into action. If we do try to "will" the raising of the limb, we shall only succeed in causing stiffness in its action. This is owing to the fact, that the raising-muscles must not commence to act, until the very moment that the *down*-action of the limb is completed, with the beginning of sound; and it is impossible for us *will-fully* to time the raising muscles with accuracy, at the very moment that the downward ones cease their work. Hence the raising-muscles must here again be taught to act only in strict *response* to the suggestion and impetus *derived from the rising key itself in its rebound*. We must therefore only think of "kicking" against the key-bed—an act analogous to the one of jumping, and the raising-muscles must act in automatic response to the felt rebound of the key; and coming thus into operation automatically, these will do so at the necessary moment. It is in this way that should be obtained this more rarely used, sharp and acrid form of Staccatissimo; and it is immaterial, in rising off the key, whether it is the finger, the hand, or the arm that is driven up.

The sharply accented initial staccato note, characteristic of a good Mazurka theme, may be cited as peculiarly appropriate for the application of this "kick-off" Staccato, and it can also be applied to staccatissimo running passages of an incisive nature. As it can be formed into an excellent test for the employment of finger-and-hand force *without* the faulty arm-force, this matter will be more fully dealt with in Chapter XVIII., "The Tests," etc.

## NOTE:

**The Nature of Glissando.**     Here is the place to point out, that the GLISSANDO is only another and even *simpler* form of "transferred Weight-touch." In this case the Weight that is to over-balance the key is applied through the back (the nail) of one finger, and the weight having reached the bed of the first key, and sounding it, this weight is then drawn along the key-board by a horizontal arm-movement. *Glissando* demands, that one or more phalanges of the finger (or fingers) employed, must be left in so gently elastic a condition, as to enable that portion of the finger to act the part of a ratchet, when the superincumbent gentle weight is drawn across the key-board. The phalanx or phalanges in question, must be sufficiently tense to permit of their supporting the Weight used *without bringing the nail too flatly* upon the keys. For unless the nail is sufficiently upright to form about *an acute angle* with the key, we cannot use it to surmount the successive keys in the required wedge-like fashion. But there must be no greater tenseness of the finger than will only just barely suffice for this purpose. Any greater tenseness, or the slightest arm-*force* applied, will inevitably jam the fingers immovably against the key-beds

   *Glissando* is therefore identical with the *ppp*-weight-transfer touch; and it even forms a most valuable and instructive channel through which to acquire the latter much-required touch, the only difference being, that in the latter case the transfer has to be effected through a sequence of fingers, in the place of the solitary one, used as a ratchet. *Crescendi*, of a limited nature, are practicable in both the Glissando and *ppp*-Transfer touch, by permitting slight increases to supervene in the resting and transferred weight,—a *continuous* weight, we must remember, in this solitary case, *without* any Added impetus. But such increments in continuously-resting weight must be but slight, and they must of course be accompanied by correspondingly slight increases in the gentle finger and hand forces applied.

A subtle variation of Species II., which forms a hybrid between Hand and Finger movement, is applicable to extremely rapid Octave-passages, such as in the Coda of the first movement of the "Waldstein" Sonata. Such passages cannot be easily performed *glissando* on the modern Piano. This hybrid touch can, however, give an almost identical effect. In it, all movement is almost entirely restricted to a movement of the fingers—to the extent of the key-depth. An extremely light glissando-like resting of the arm is thus caused to mount the successive keys, almost as in the true glissando.

The Three Chief Muscular Tests.

(Chapter XVIII.)

RECAPITULATORY.

*a):* Knowledge of what constitutes correct muscular action and in-action at the Piano, proves that three points of muscular efficiency are of paramount necessity:

*b):*
> I. We must learn to *rest* properly on the keys, by leaving our fingers and hands free from contrary exertion, when they are applied to the keys.
>
> II. We must learn accurately to *time* the culmination and the *cessation* of the energy we apply to move the key.
>
> III. We must acquire the power to *use* our fingers and hands quite independently of any downward-acting arm-force, and even independently of arm-weight.

*c):* We must *test* ourselves constantly during Practice and Performance, so that we may ensure compliance with these paramount necessities.[1]

*d):* The Three Muscular-tests required, are as follows:

Test I  To ensure proper Resting, and use of the Muscular-sense; by freeing the finger and hand from contrary-exertions; two Exs.·—

I): Employ a slight up-and-down balancing movement of the arm at the Wrist; the hand to lie loose, and the fingers to remain in contact with their respective keys. See to it, that no alteration occurs in the Weight resting on the keys, which must remain at their surface-level.

---

[1] As these tests form preventives of wrong-doing, they should invariably be practised the first thing every day

2): Roll and unroll the fingers by means of a for·
ward and backward movement of the arm and hand,
while the finger-tips remain unaffected thereby, both as to
position and as to the Resting-weight, as before.[1]

**Test II. To ensure proper " aiming " of the Added-impetus ; accuracy in
Tone-production :—**

Play an easy chord (preferably by " weight " or clinging-touch[2]), and accurately *cease* all action of the finger and
hand the moment that Sound is reached, so as to allow the
Wrist to *drop* in consequence. The weight used, must
also disappear in consequence of the cessation of its support at the wrist. The keys will thus be able to *rebound*
of their own accord, in spite of the finger-tips resting on
their surfaces, and in spite of the descending wrist and
arm.[3] See to it, that the resulting *staccato* is absolute,
both when practised *pp* and when practised *ff*.

**Test III. To ensure elimination of Down-arm-exertion, and independence of
the finger-and-hand exertions, even from arm-weight :—**

Play a short run or arpeggio, and drive the arm off
the keys, in accenting the last note ; using a kind of kick
against the key-bed, delivered for the purpose by the finger and hand. The key to *rebound* (forming *staccatissimo*)
and to seem to drive the arm into the air.[4]

This, also to be practised *pianissimo*, without the final accent.
The arm, in this case seems to *float* upwards, instead of being
driven off.

[1] Any alteration in the degree of Weight forms presumptive proof that
contrary-exertions have been permitted ; so does any forward or backward
sliding of the finger-tips on the key-surfaces. No alteration occurs in either of
these respects, if the contrary-muscles of both Hand and Finger are left as relaxed as they should be

[2] N. B —The weight required for " Clinging-touch " must be obtained by
release of the *upper* arm

[3] If practised instead with " forward " or thrusting-touch, the wrist will
not fall, but will rebound upwards—but the fingers must nevertheless remain
on their respective keys, with the rising keys under them.

[4] This test should be practised in two ways : (a) with the whole arm rising
in the air, and (b) with the fore-arm alone, thus responding to the rebound of
the keys.

*e*): Rotary and lateral freedom at the Wrist, should also constantly be *tested* for. This, by allowing the resulting movements to continue during the moment of key-depression and beyond that moment. Both kinds of movement to be perfectly free from all restraint.

---

## THE THREE SPECIES OF TOUCH-FORMATION.

*o*

### (CHAPTER XIX.)

### RECAPITULATORY.

*a*): We have learnt that the three muscular-components available (Finger-force, Hand-force, and Arm-weight with its coöperatives) can be applied to the Key, under three main Principles of Combination, forming three distinct Species of Touch-formation:

Description of the Three Species of Touch-formation:

*b*): The First Species consists of Finger-force alone acting against the key during descent; while the hand is passive, and the Arm self-supported.

The Second Species consists of Hand-force acting in conjunction with the Finger against the key during descent; while the Arm remains self-supported.

The Third Species consists of all three components, operative

against the key during descent; Finger and Hand force being
supplemented by Arm-weight, etc.

How these Touch-formations are used :

*c*) : To produce the 1st Species : the Arm must remain fully
but elastically supported by its own muscles, and while the Arm
thus floats over the key-board and supports the Wrist-end of the
loose-lying Hand, the sound must be produced solely by the
Finger's action against the key ; such Finger-action ceasing the
moment that sound is reached.

*d*) · To produce the 2d Species : the Arm-condition is the same
as in the last, but the Hand must here act behind the Finger
during key-descent : both Finger and Hand accurately ceasing to
act, the moment that sound is heard to begin.

*e*) : To produce the 3d Species : we have to add Arm-weight
behind the Finger and Hand, the latter acting as in the other
Species.  Such lapse in Arm-support must reach its climax at
the moment of sound-emission, and it, as well as the finger-and-
hand actions employed, must disappear at that very moment.

The forms of Movement available :

*f*) : The Third Species can be employed either in the form of
Arm-touch (arm-movement), or Hand-touch [1] (Hand-movement),
or as Finger-touch (Finger-movement) ; all three forms of movement being available in this Species, since it contains all the
three muscular-components.

The Second Species can only be employed either in the form
of Hand-touch or as Finger-touch, since the Arm does not here
change its condition during the act of tone-production.

The First Species is only available as Finger-touch, since
neither Hand nor Arm should here show any change of condition
during key-descent.

The speeds at which the Species are available :

*g*) : The Third Species can however only be used, when the
speed of the passage does not exceed a certain rate ;—the speed

[1] " Wrist-action."

being restricted by the limit beyond which we cannot give the necessary repetitions of Arm-release.[1]

The Second Species permits far greater Agility, while——

The First Species offers no physical limit to speed, beyond the mental difficulty of keeping the passage " in hand."

The contrasts of Tone-*quantity* available :

b) : The Third Species offers us the whole range of Tone, from the very softest to the loudest and fullest, owing to the presence of Arm-weight.

The Second Species cannot procure us so much Tone, as the Hand and Finger here have only the self-supported (or suspended) Arm as a Basis.

The First Species only renders a very small quantity of Tone available, since we here have only the slight weight of the loose-lying Hand as a Basis.

The contrasts of Tone-*quality* available :

i) : The *Third* is the only Species, under which all varieties of Tone-*quality* are available. For it is owing to the inclusion of Arm-release, that we can under this Species *start* the act of Tone-production either by Weight-release or by Muscular-exertion. [2]

The Second and First Species only permit " Muscular-initiative." No " singing " tone can therefore be obtained through them.

j) : All three Species can moreover be somewhat modified (either towards Beauty or towards Harshness) by selecting either the flat (or clinging) attitude, or the bent (or thrusting) attitude.

k) : To obtain fully " sympathetic " *cantabile* or *cantando*, we must combine the Clinging-attitude with the Third Species, in its Weight-initiative form.

[1] Such alternations of Arm-release and renewed self-support, are, we must remember, not necessarily shown as arm-*movements*.
What may be considered a Variety of this Species, is, however, also available in full-speed passages, provided we do not attempt to obtain more tone than a *piano*—provided, therefore, that it takes the form of ' transfer" (or " passing-on ") touch    In this form it is also available as a GLISSANDO
[2] We must remember that with " Weight-touch " the tendency is towards beauty of tone, while with "Muscular-touch " it is towards hardness, harshness (or asperity) of quality.

Bent finger, 2d Species, compulsory, for rapid *forte* passages.

*l) :* We moreover now discern, that the Clinging (or flat) finger, requires some measure of Upper-arm release. This incapacitates this form of touch for *rapid* passages, when these are required *forte.*

For rapid *forte* passages, we must therefore use the self-supported arm (Second Species) with the thrusting (or bent) finger in combination with it.[1]

*m) :* The secret of Agility, hence, is found to lie in the self-supported arm ; and combined with it, the thrusting finger, when the passage is *forte.* Accuracy in ceasing the action *at* sound, is a law that meanwhile bears no breaking.

The contrasts in Duration, how available :

*n) :* All three Species of touch-formation are Staccato, provided we insist meanwhile on the Act of Resting being sufficiently light ;—so light that the arm is continuously in a state of complete self-support; and provided we are also careful to time our *actions against* the keys to *cease* so accurately as to permit these to rebound.[2]

*o) :* All the Species can be transformed into Tenuti, by merely changing the Resting into a slightly heavier form, the arm (as to its *continuous* condition) being here not quite so fully supported as in Staccato.

*p) :* All the Species can moreover be transformed into Legati, by transferring such Tenuto-form of the Resting from key to key.

The danger of forgetting to think of Sound, when learning new muscular habits :

*q) :* In endeavouring to acquire correct Muscular-conditions, we must meanwhile never lose sight of their Object, *viz.:* to *move* the Key *for the sake* of Music.

---

[1] The clinging-finger, would in rapid *forte* passages, tend to dull the passage by dragging the Upper-arm on to the key-beds

[2] We must recall that the *Continuous* condition of the arm, here implied in the Resting, does by no means preclude our using the momentary lapses required in Species III , to form the Added-impetus.

To succeed in this, we must remember to watch the key un-remittingly, both before depression—for its weight, and during depression—for the Place where tone-production culminates and ceases.   We can moreover only ensure our doing this, by remembering to watch TIME.

We must therefore insist on judging not only how, but *where* each note should sound.   Thus, only, can we hope to learn to employ Technique solely for a Musical Purpose.

*r) :* The following Table should now be studied.

# TABLE SHOWING RELATIONSHIP BETWEEN THE THREE SPECIES OF ADDED-IMPETUS, MOVEMENT, AND THE RESTING, Etc.

## THE ACT OF ADDED-IMPETUS :

— required during the moment of key-descent for all tone-making, except *ppp*-ten. and leg., and *always as short-lived as in staccatissimo*:—

| FIRST SPECIES. | SECOND SPECIES. | THIRD SPECIES. | |
|---|---|---|---|
| — Momentary finger-exertion alone, with lax hand and self-supported arm. | — Momentary hand-exertion behind the finger-exertion, with self-supported arm. | — Momentary Arm-weight release behind finger-and-hand exertion. | |
| | | (a) WEIGHT-initiated.* | (b) MUSCU-LARLY-initiated.‡ |

**MOVEMENTS AVAILABLE :—**

| | | |
|---|---|---|
| Finger-touches only. | Finger-touches and Hand (Wrist) touches. | Finger-touches, Hand-touches, and Arm=touches.‡ |

**FINGER-ARM ATTITUDES AVAILABLE :—**

{ (a) The " flat," or Clinging — — — helps towards sympathetic quality.
{ (b) The " bent," or Thrusting — — — helps towards brilliant quality.

## THE ACT OF RESTING :

— required continuously during each phrase :—

(A): The *Staccato* Basis, at Surface key-level :— { Hand-weight only, — — — insufficient to depress keys, or to retain them depressed.

(B): The *Tenuto* or *Legato* Basis, at Depressed key-level :— { Arm-weight §, sufficient, unassisted, to induce key-descent for *ppp-*tenuto and legato.

* Makes for thick tone.  † Makes for sharp tone.  ‡ Including arm-rotation touches.  § The *whole* arm, slightly released continuously.

84

CLASSIFICATION OF TOUCHES.

(CHAPTER XX.)

## RECAPITULATORY AND SUMMARY.

*a)* : Enumeration and Classification only become possible (and easy) if we bear in mind the main facts of Touch-construction, *viz.*:—

1) : The Resting.

2) : The Added-impetus.

3) : The Three distinct Species of muscular-combination, or Touch-formation ; and

4) : The two great distinctions thence elicited :

I.) : *Weight*-initiated Touch.

II.) : *Muscularly*-initiated Touch.

5) : The Distinction between Clinging and Thrusting attitudes.

*b)* : To attain our present object, we must review some of the potentialities of these Elements :

1) : The *Third* Species of Muscular-combination (or Touch-formation) alone offers us (because of its two Sub-genera) the option both of Muscular-initiative and of Weight-initiative; the other Species being necessarily Muscularly-initiated.

This *Third* Species, as regards movement, can be exhibited either as Finger-touch, Hand-touch, or as Arm-touch.

2) : The *Second* Species only offers the option between Finger-touch and Hand-touch.

3) : The *First* Species can only be obtained as Finger-touch.

4) : The *Thrusting* and *Clinging* muscular-attitudes tend to qualify *all* Touch towards the Brilliant type and towards the Sympathetic type, respectively.

5) : The *whole* of these Tone-producing Elements can be applied either under the *first* (Key-surface) form of

the Resting, or under the *second* (Key-depressed) form of the Resting :

In the first case the effect is STACCATO; and in the second case it is TENUTO, and the latter can, moreover, in the case of Finger-touch, be transformed into Legato.

6) : The *Second* form of the Resting, applied by itself to the key (without the assistance of any Added-impetus) forms the true *pp*-tenuto or Legato—*pp* Weight-touch or Transfer-touch.

It is identical with the muscular-combination, Species III., and can therefore exist either in the guise of Finger, Hand, or Arm-movement.[1]

*c ) :* From the Artist's point of view—and the Student-*colourist's*[2]—Classification must therefore needs take the following aspect :

| | |
|---|---|
| Div.    I. : Weight *v.* Muscular-initiative.<br>Div.   II. : Flat *v.* Bent Finger-arm Attitude (Clinging *v.* Thrusting). | Forming the distinctions of tone-*quality* · roundness *v* hardness, or Sympathetic *v* Aggressive. |
| Div. III. : The Three Species of Added-impetus-construction    .. | Giving various options of tone-*quantity*, and Agility-powers. |
| Div. IV. : Key-surface *v.* key-bed Resting ..    . . ..    ........ . | Forming the distinctions between Legato and Staccato |
| and lastly, | |
| Div.  V. : Finger, Hand, and Arm-touches. | Forming the distinctions of mere movement |

*d ) :* Subsidiary modifications are :—

1) : An additional set of touch-forms, exhibited as Fore-arm Rotation-touch, sometimes advisable, and available under most forms of touch-construction.

---

[1] This Resting, when applied in conjunction with a 1st Species Added-impetus, subtly modifies the latter's tone-quality.

[2] Without *Colouring*, Piano-playing is reduced to mere strumming.

2): The "Kick-off" Staccato influence; capable of being added to all the enumerated forms of Staccato.

3): The "Artificial" form of Legato, induced by slight and continuous pressure of the hand and fingers, in place of the usual heavier form of the Resting.

*e)*: All these distinctions need not be consciously kept in view, once we have mastered their application. But we must more or less remain conscious of those few *main principles* recalled in §§ *a* and *c* of this Recapitulatory.

*f)*: The following Table should now be referred to.

# FINAL CLASSIFICATION.

TONE-QUALITY is here the basis of Classification. It is the one that should be kept in view both by the Performer and Student-Colourist.

| DIVISION I. WEIGHT-TOUCH. (Makes for Roundness of tone.) | DIVISION II. MUSCULAR-TOUCH. (Makes for Brilliancy of tone.) |
|---|---|
| Obtained *solely* under: (a) SPECIES III, in its 1st Sub-genus—Weight-release initiated, and (b) *Second* form of the *Resting* when employed unaided. | Obtained under either: Species I, Species II, or Species III, in its 2nd Sub-genus—Muscularly-initiated. |

Both Divisions may be further modified, either towards Beauty, or towards Aggressiveness of tone, by the "Clinging" attitude and the "Thrusting" attitude, respectively.

Both may be accompanied either by: (a) The STACCATO Basis—The Resting at Surface-level of Key-board,* or (b) The TENUTO and LEGATO Basis—The Resting at depressed-level of Key-board.†

Can be exhibited under the following aspects of Movement:**

| a: Finger-touch. | b: Hand (Wrist) touch. | c: Arm-touch. | a: Finger-touch. Formed either under: 1st *Species*, 2nd *Species*, or 3rd *Species*, in its 2nd Sub-genus. | b: Hand (Wrist) touch. Formed either under: 2nd *Species*, or 3rd *Species*, in its 2nd Sub-genus. | c: Arm-touch. Formed under: 3rd *Species*, in its 2nd Sub-genus. |
|---|---|---|---|---|---|

* Or with addition of "Kick-off."    † Or with addition or alternative of "Pressure-legato" element.    ** Also as Rotation-touch.

# RECAPITULATORY AND SUMMARY

OF THE MAIN CONCLUSIONS OF

## PART III

**The Link.[1]** 1) : During the process of learning the requisite Muscular-habits (when we must of necessity pay attention to the muscular-details) we must not permit this to divert our attention from the *instrument's* requirements; these must always be kept supremely in view, and for the sake of the required musical-effect. That is: Muscular-action must only be thought of—and applied—for the purpose of fulfilling the requirements of the key, and these again solely for the purpose of Musical-result.

2) : The key's requirements vary according to each difference in sound-shading dictated by our musical sense. Accurate and musical Technique hence demands that our muscular-efforts must vary correspondingly.

3) : We can only insure this correspondence by an unswerving attention to the RESISTANCE the keys offer before and during descent. We must therefore constantly notice the "giving-way point" of the key, even in the case of our employing a considerable movement before reaching it.

4) : Attention thus given through our resistance-sense, also enforces Musical-attention and intention; for we find ourselves compelled to refer to our musical-conscience, the moment we endeavour to judge what should be done to each key.

**On Key-Contact.[2]** 5) : It follows, that *Key-contact* must never take the form of a real blow, if we desire musical-accuracy.

[1] For explanation of §§ 2 to 4, refer to Chapter XIII., page 114.
[2] Explanation of §§ 5 to 7, found in Chapter XIV., page 125.
  *N B.— These references are always to " The Act of Touch "*

6) : Not only should we therefore reach the key-surface quite easily and lightly; but we must also be most careful to remember, that the required tone has to be made during the ensuing short descending *movement* of the key.[1]

7) : This light fall of the limb upon, and subsequent movement with the key, may either form an unbroken descent, or we may instead bring the finger into contact with the key before the moment its depression is due.        But in either case we must, before using the key, insist on feeling its resistance.

---

*Concepts of Touch.[2]*        8) : Since careful Contact is so essential, and since Tenuto and Legato further require the operation of a light resting Weight, and as we must nevertheless often apply much energy to the key in addition to this Resting to provoke the key into the necessary tone, it follows that TOUCH consists of the combination of two muscular operations, *viz.* :

a) The act of "Resting," and
b) The act of "Added-impetus."

9) : The act of "Resting" is practically continuous during each phrase, but may differ in its actual weight. This constitutes the difference in Basis between Staccato and Legato.

10) : The "Added-impetus" is applied only for and during key-descent; and it must cease to exist the very moment that tone-emission commences.        This law applies both in Legato and in Staccato.

11) : For *Staccato,* the Resting must be no heavier than the key will bear at its top-most level.

For *Tenuto* and *Legato,* the Resting should never be heavier than will just suffice to retain the keys depressed.

12) : The Legato-resting, employed without any Added-impetus, is the only simple form of touch; and thus employed, it gives us an absolute *ppp* Tenuto or Legato.

---

[1] For the act of Tone-production does not really *commence* until we have actually reached the key.
[2] Explanation of §§ 8 to 15, found in Chapter XV., page 135.

13) : Legato implies a sequence of complete Tenuti, transferred from finger to finger.

14) : *Duration* therefore depends on the kind of Resting. while *Sound-kind* depends on the kind of Added-impetus.

---

The limbs and
their muscles.[1]

15) : Four distinct living-levers are employed, *viz.:* the Finger, the Hand, the Fore-arm, and the Upper-arm.

16) : The finger itself can be exerted in two completely different ways:

    *a)* The Bent, or *thrusting* attitude, and

    *b)* The Flat, or *clinging* attitude.[2]

17) : By means of attached muscles, we can exert any of these living-levers in many directions.

18) : Moreover, for every direction in which we can thus exert these levers, we can also exert them in the opposite direction, by means of opposite muscles.

19) : *Stiffness* is induced, when we exert both these sets of muscles simultaneously.    We must therefore carefully guard against doing this ; for unless we provide every required action and movement with perfect freedom, we shall certainly spoil all our playing.

---

The Actions
and In-actions.[3]

20) : The muscular-operation against the key implies leverage on the part of the finger and hand.

This leverage re-acts upwards: (a) against the hand at the knuckle, and (b) against the arm at the wrist.

21) : To form the necessary Basis, the arm may be employed in two ways: (a) it may be fully self-supported by its own muscles, or (b) its *weight* may be set free by relaxation, during each act of key-depression.[4]

---

[1] Explanation of §§ 16 to 19, found in Chapter XVI , page 147.
[2] *Vide Figs  6 and 7.*
[3] Explanation of §§ 20 to 43 are found in Chapter XVII., page 158.
[4] For extreme *fortes*, in addition to the full use of arm-weight, we may lever the weight of the shoulder on to the key.

22) : The sensation of exertion is always *upwards* in correct touch, since the required exertions should be mainly derived from finger-and-hand leverage—which by reaction from the keys operates upwards against knuckle and wrist.[1]

23) : There are three main *muscular-components* : Finger and Hand down-exertion, and Arm-weight.

24) : *Loudness* depends on the total degree of Energy thus derived.

25) : *Quality* mainly depends on the locality of the initiatory muscular-component;—*i.e.* : whether we start the act of key-depression by Muscular-initiative or Weight-initiative. The first makes for sudden key-depression—sharpness of tone; whereas the second makes for that gradual attainment of key-speed associated with beauty of tone.

26) : *Quality* is moreover modified in these same directions, by the contrast obtainable between the Thrusting and the Clinging finger-attitudes, and their related upper-arm conditions;—*i.e.* : by the contrast between a forward-held, or a backward-hanging Elbow.[2]

27) : To obtain the extreme effects of Quality, we must *combine* both of these influences.

28) : The most active portion of the finger should always be that next to the knuckle of the hand. This applies equally in Thrusting and in Clinging touch.

29) : *Movement*—the distinction between Finger-touch, Hand-touch, and Arm-touch—depends upon which one of the three muscular-*components*[3] is slightly in excess of the other two, during the process of key-speeding (descent).

30) : Choice of *Movement* should be mainly determined by the speed of the passage. Finger-movement (Finger-touch), however, can be employed both in quick and in slow passages.

31) : Good choice of *Touch-formation*—or Species of touch—

[1] The reaction is upwards against the shoulder in extreme cases.
[2] *Vide Figs. 8 and 9, page 166; Fig 10, page 167; and Figs. 12 and 13, page 171.*
[3] Finger-force, Hand-force, and Arm-weight.

is nevertheless far more important, since upon it depends the kind and degree of tone, and our agility-possibilities.

32) : There are three ways of forming or constructing the act of Touch from its three muscular-components. These three muscular-*combinations* are :—(a) *First Species of Touch-formation*, Finger-exertion only, with passive hand and self-supported arm; (b) *Second Species of Touch-formation*, Hand and finger exertions, combined with the self-supported arm; (c) *Third Species of Touch-formation*, Arm-weight employed in conjunction with the exertions of the finger and hand.

33) : Arm-weight, whenever it is employed,[1] must be obtained by releasing or relaxing the arm-supporting muscles. The *whole* arm from the shoulder must thus be relaxed, to the extent required by the key; and we must guard against endeavouring to obtain the required weight from the Fore-arm only.

34) : The slight but *continuous* release of Arm-weight which induces the second (or slightly heavier) form of the Resting—and which forms the basis of all natural Tenuti and Legati, is identical with the act of tone-production at its very *softest*.
To obtain this effect, we must release arm-weight upon the key, until the latter's resistance is just overcome. The consequent sinking down of the key feels more like a passive process than like an active one.

35) : Arm-weight, when applied as an "Added-impetus," must cease to operate against the key the very moment that sound is reached. This cessation must be wrought by accurately timing the hand-and-finger exertions against the key. And it is in response to the consequent disappearance of support at the Wrist that the arm-supporting muscles must be automatically called into action.

36) : Natural Legato arises, when we transfer the second form of the "Resting" from finger to finger. The result is *ppp*, unless we meanwhile add force in some form during key-depression;—*i.e.* : unless we also employ the Added-impetus in one of its numberless forms.

[1] Both in its forms of "Added-impetus" and of "Resting."

37) : Such transfer of the Resting-weight must also occur *automatically*—*i.e. :* in response to the cessation of the *last* finger's supporting action upon the key; this being timed to occur at the moment the *next* finger's key is desired to commence its descent.

38) : For the Staccato-form of the "Resting," the weight of the hand is found sufficient, and this is not ponderous enough to prevent the required rebound of the key.

39) : We must remember that the "Added-impetus" is quite as short-lived in Tenuto and Legato as it is in Staccatissimo.

40) : The fore-arm *Rotation*-element is extremely important. To it we owe our possibilities of Evenness of Touch, and also the power to render notes prominent at either side of the hand. The adjustments in question must therefore be constant, although for the most part invisible.

This adjustment, when it is allowed to become visible as an actual tilting of the hand, is termed *Rotation-touch*

41) : Lateral freedom of the Wrist and Hand is imperative. Free horizontal movements of the hand are also required to promote evenness, when turning over the thumb and turning under the fingers.

42) : "Wrist-freedom," which is so much desired by everyone, must hence be insisted upon in all these three aspects—the vertical, rotary and horizontal. We can insure such freedom by insisting on *feeling vertical* over each key, before commencing to use it.

43) : Subsidiary points are:—freedom in the horizontal movements of the fore-arm itself, and of the fingers, and of the upper-arm, when bringing the finger-tips over their respective keys.

---

Muscular Testing [1]    44) : Three Muscular Tests are essential, so that we may insure our fulfilling the required Muscular Conditions. These tests, which should be practised every day before anything else, are as follows:

45) : *Test No. I. :* —A slight up-and-down swaying of the

[1] Explanations of §§ 44 to 47, found in Chapter XVIII., page 204.

Wrist-joint, while the finger-tips remain lying on their keys; also a rolling and un-rolling of the fingers themselves, while they support a certain proportion of the weight of the hand on the keys. Designed to insure the elimination of all *contrary* exertions from those required from the finger and the hand.

46): *Test No. II.*:—A drop of the Wrist-joint, occurring in response to the accurately-timed cessation of the finger-and-hand exertion, at the moment of sound-emission; thus permitting the keys to rebound while the Wrist falls past them. Designed to secure accuracy in " aiming" the act of Tone-production. This should be practised in four ways: Staccato, *pp* and *ff; Legato, pp* and *ff*.

47): *Test No. III:*—The performance of a short, light run, ending in a rebound of the arm off the keys with the last note; practised (a) with the whole arm thus rebounding, and (b) with the fore-arm alone thus rebounding; and practised both with a vigorous bounding-off and with a gentle floating-off of the arm. Designed to insure the elimination of Down-arm-force from the required down-exertions of the finger and the hand.

---

The Three Species of Touch-formation [1]   48): All three species can be applied as "Added-impetus" both during Legato and during Staccato.

49): *The First Species* can only be applied through finger-*movement*—" finger-touch." It enables us to provide the highest degrees of Agility, but it offers us only slight possibilities of Tone-contrast.

50): *The Second Species* can be applied both as Finger-touch and as Hand-touch—"Wrist-touch." It enables us to provide greater contrasts in tone-*quantity* than the first species, but agility-power is here more restricted.

51): *The Third Species* can be applied in all three forms of Movement; *viz.*: as Finger-touch, Hand-touch, and as Arm-touch. This species permits us to attain not only the fullest contrasts in Tone-quantity, but also those of Tone-*quality*.

[1] Explanation of §§ 48 to 52, found in Chapter XIX., page 214.

Agility is however still more limited, owing to the rapid alternations of arm-release and re-support here required.

52) : We must bear in mind the particular scope (the possibilities and limitations) of these Three Species, when we (consciously or un-consciously) choose the touch-formation for each particular passage; we may otherwise fail to employ the most appropriate form.

---

Enumeration        53) : Enumeration and Classification are possible,
and Classifica-  if we recall the main facts of Touch-construction.
tion of          We thus find there are some 42 distinct kinds of
Touches.[1]      key-attack, as follows:

54) : *Finger-staccato, eight kinds :*—for we can employ either the 1st Species of touch-formation, or the 2nd, or the 3rd, and the latter in either of its two aspects (either as Weight-touch or as Muscular-touch), and we can employ these four either as Clinging or as Thrusting-touch.

55) : *Finger-legato, ten kinds :*—for we have the same options as in Finger-Staccato, and have in addition the option of using the Resting unaided (*ppp* Ten., or Leg.) either under the Bent or Flat finger conditions.

56) : *Hand (wrist) staccato, six kinds :*—in the form either of 2nd Species, or 3rd Species under its two aspects, and these again either as Clinging or Thrusting-touch.

57) : *Hand (wrist) tenuto, eight kinds :*—the same options as in Hand-staccato, and in addition, the Bent and Flat finger forms of the un-aided Resting.

58) : *Arm-staccato, four kinds :*—3rd Species either in its muscularly-initiated or weight-initiated form, and these taken either Bent or Flat.

59) : *Arm-tenuto, six kinds :*—the same alternatives as with Arm-staccato, but with the additional ones obtained under the unaided Resting, with either thrusting or clinging key-attack.

60) : From the Artist's and Colourist's point of view, Classifi-

[1] Explanation of §§ 53 to 60, found in Chapter XX., page 238.

cation is as follows:—*Weight*-touch and *Muscular*-touch; these under *Flat* or *Bent* attitudes; these all under any of the *Three Species* of Touch-formation; these again under the two alternatives of *Resting*, with their Staccato or Legato result; and finally all these under the aspect of *movement*—either **Arm,** or **Hand,** or **Finger**-touch.

# NOTES TO PART III.

### CERTAIN EXCEPTIONAL FORMS OF STACCATO AND LEGATO, AND THE SLIGHTLY HEAVIER RESTING THUS TRANSMISSIBLE

NOTE XVII.—For Note to § 28, Chapter XVII, page 186  Slightly more Weight than has been described under the two forms of the Resting, can under certain exceptional conditions be continuously applied in finger-passages, both Staccato and Legato  That is, the fingers can carry such slightly-increased load without harm, provided the speed of the passage is considerable, and yet does not exceed a certain limit, and provided moreover, that the individual fingers are used with sufficient vigour in forming the short-lived " Added impetuses " against the keys;—for the exceptionally vigorous momentary action of the fingers, will in this case *prevent* such additional weight from actually *reaching the key-beds*  The process is analogous to the action of the legs in running for in this case our body is kept floating off the ground by the rapid succession of jump-like acts delivered against it by the legs—a fact that can easily be demonstrated by Snap-shot camera

In such exceptional touches, we can therefore employ a slightly increased weight (or slight hand-pressure as the case may be) borne by the successive fingers, and as it were *kept floating* (away from the key-beds) by the aforesaid sharp, individually-aimed (and ceased) exertions of the fingers.  The weight (or pressure) must however never be greater than the fingers can thus keep in a "floating" condition, by the rapid succession of their momentary " kicks " or impacts against the key-beds  Provided the Weight thus carried does not exceed a soon discovered limit, we thus obtain a running form of the " kick-off " Staccato, already described, this is suitable for certain bright, brisk, but *forte* Staccato-passages.

By a slightly different adjustment of the continuous weight *versus* the briskly stepping finger, this kind of technique can be transformed into a softer but *legato* form, or even into a Legatissimo, such as we often meet with in BEETHOVEN.

The extra weight thus continuously carried, might preferably in this case be provided by a *slight, continuous activity of the Hand and Fingers*, rather than by any extra arm-release  For the slight continuous *pressure*, thus produced by the hand and fingers, levers arm-weight continuously on to the keys at will, and the weight is thus more directly and momentarily modifiable, and more elastic, than would be the case did we relax the arm sufficiently to obtain the full amount of weight necessary to induce the effect of *Super-legato*, for instance.  This gentle, added Hand-pressure is therefore particularly suitable to induce the over-lapping of the sounds required in the super-legato inflections of Legato  We here have the "artificial" legato, already several times referred to.  To distinguish this from the natural, or Weight-legato, it might be termed a "*pressure*-legato."

No passage should however be attempted in this form of technique unless the speed is ample to admit of such " pressure " being kept in the floating state described, otherwise stickiness is bound to ensue  The cumbrousness of it, also precludes the employment of this form of technique beyond a soon-reached limit of velocity.

Besides the possibility of thus producing Legatissimo inflections by slight Hand-pressures, we may also in similar manner produce such inflections by slight pressures, sufficiently continued, but derived *from the fingers* alone. Such un-aided finger-*pressures*, are the ones most suitable for the legatissimo inflections of *light* running passages.

The truth will here become clearer to us, how all extreme Agility-key-treatment must as a matter of fact be purely STACCATO Owing, however, to the extreme speed employed, the Ear cannot detect any Staccato, since the "damping" of the instrument cannot be prompt enough to permit any actual separation being exhibited between the sounds, when they occur in such close succession. In practising such passages slowly, it is therefore futile to practise them Legato, since the attainment of the desired speed depends so materially upon the accuracy of their Staccato production.

In this connection it behoves us to remember, that the Wrist-joint must ever remain absolutely free and flexible ,—in proper touch there should never be sufficient down-pressure upon it, to prevent its being so In the *first* two species of technique (where the finger and hand alone act against the key, while the arm remains self-supported) the Wrist joint is indeed in a condition so elastic, that it is *almost* on the point of being driven off the keys by the rapidly recurring, short-lived actions of the finger and hand against the keys—whence we see the reason for insisting on the constant practice of the *third* of the "Muscular-tests" described in Chapter XVIII. The wrist should consequently feel as if it were *floating in space*, in spite of the perhaps quite vigorous finger-and-hand exertions against the individual keys, —exertions, which must of course be so fleeting, and must be so carefully timed in all Agility touches as to vanish before they induce the slightest impeding action against the key-*beds*

We can in fact often suggest the correct muscular-attitude here required, by simply insisting upon the Wrist-joint remaining absolutely free,—*free almost to the rebounding point*, as just described, owing to the upward-recoil kicks received by it at each sound-consummation. It is also well to remember, that all action must here seem to *end* either at the Knuckle, or at the Wrist-end of the hand,—such action being there felt as an up-driving one, from the keys upwards against the knuckle and wrist,—and such action being individualised for each sound, and as short-lived as the shortest Staccatissimo always proves the act of tone-production to be in its nature.

## *IN-CORRECT VERSUS CORRECT FINGER-TECHNIQUE*

### *The Contrast between the Non individualised and the Individualised Finger.*

NOTE XVI —To §§ 4 and 18, Chapter XVII. The distinction here in question, is the one between (a) "stickiness" of finger, with its un-rhythmical passages, and (b) fluency and ease of finger, with its clean-cut, rhythmically definite passages—with every note perfectly " placed " and evenly sounded.

The point that should be enforced, is, that the fault can usually be traced to the employment of defective *muscular-conditions*, which in their turn render it impossible for the sufferer wilfully to direct his fingers in quick passages, either as regards Time or Tone.

The muscular fault in such cases is the one so often here alluded to and condemned,—the use of continuous Arm-*pressure* behind the fingers.  It is, we must remember, the most natural fault to make —We wish to make the key before us move down,—what more natural, than that we should try to induce this by using the muscles of the back, with down-pressure of the arm ? If we wished to press down anything in the ordinary course of our existence, we should certainly act thus, and rightly so   At the Piano the temptation to act likewise is commensurately great, and it *must at any cost* be resisted   This tendency must indeed he absolutely eliminated, if we wish to succeed in play-ing passages with ease, and wish to avoid liability to a sudden and com-plete collapse of our Technique, when the moment of stress arrives.  How often do we find an otherwise admirable performer, suddenly lose all clean-ness and fluency of finger !  An unduly felted or over-toned hammer is per-haps presented for his use, and being thus prevented from *hearing* what a con-siderable degree of force he is already applying to the keys, he endeavours to apply more,—and he will then be tempted to transgress the laws of finger-technique, and will permit himself to apply that fatal thing, Arm-pressure, unless the laws of Agility have been fixed into secure habit of mind and body.  If these laws are ignored, the passages go from bad to worse, until they become almost obliterated under the more and more laboured progress that ensues upon the key *beds*, and the performer leaves the instrument with perspiration streaming from him, and feeling as if he had suffered under the incubus of a nightmare.

The fault of all faults to be guarded against is therefore · a continuous PRESSURE exerted downwards upon the fingers by the arm , a condition of affairs that renders the hand as helpless as if it were a *hoof*, with five prongs attached, instead of fingers.  If such pressure is *continuous, and at all severe*, it absolutely stops all movement across the key-board.        To help one to avoid this fault, one should commit it deliberately, doing so in a scale or arpeggio; so that its sensation of stickiness may be vividly experienced, and so that its unfailing result, the complete breakdown of all technique may be as vividly remembered.

Less obvious than this *continuous* arm-pressure, is the occasionally at-tempted correction of it.  Many a musician, with even mediocre reasoning power, will soon learn to avoid the *continuous* effort behind the fingers just condemned, since he finds himself thereby deprived of all Agility.  But this will not prevent his using the same muscular-combination (*i e* , direct down-arm force behind his fingers) when he wishes to play *forte* finger-passages, provided he now carefully *ceases such force* the moment that tone is reached with each key.        And many a player's technique never advances beyond this stage, since it enables him to "get along" somehow, and even at consid-erable speed        Naturally enough, he will fail to recognise his inefficiency technically, unless his ears are sufficiently quick to detect, that other (and better) players are able to play similar passages with greater ease, and with far *more beautiful tone ,*—or unless he some day, by lucky accident, happens to discover the correct technique,—and is able to recognise it as such at the moment

No, the arm must neither be continuously pressed down upon the fingers, nor may it be "jabbed" down on them for each individual note.  There must be none of this, in any shape whatsoever !

The only forms of technique that will permit of the attainment of real Agility, are those two forms in both of which the arm is almost or entirely supported off the keys by its own muscles—the *first* and the *second* Species of Touch-formation ; and, either in conjunction with these, or unaided, the Weight-transfer touch—or second form of the act of Resting — *Vide Chapter XIX.*

# EXTRACT.

## PART IV.

### ON POSITION.

# PART IV.

## ON POSITION.

### THE DETAILS OF POSITION.

#### PREAMBLE.

MOST of the details of Position have already been fully dealt with in Part III., under the aspect of muscular action and inaction. In addition, it has been pointed out in the last chapter, that there are certain of these details of Position that require careful watching. For the sake of completeness, however, it is now desirable to go over the whole ground from its positional aspect. In doing this, we must not forget, that correct Position should be but the natural result of the fulfilment of the exact muscular-conditions required by correct Key-treatment, and that we must beware of falling into the error of regarding Position, itself, as the cause of correct touch.

Understanding then thoroughly, that correct position is no guarantee whatever that the essential muscular-conditions are being satisfactorily promoted, and that the subject of Position is only important in so far, that inaccuracy in this respect does render it more difficult to provide these correct conditions, the fact nevertheless remains that the study of Position is indeed important, although not so important as has been popularly supposed, and although it is certainly not one of those "short cuts" to the top of Mount Parnassus, so beloved of the amateur reasoner.

# RECAPITULATORY

OF CHAPTER XXIII., AND OF

## PART IV

*Finger, verti-*
*cally consid-*
*ered.*

1): Two quite distinct positions of the finger are available. The difference between the two is more noticeable when the finger is raised than when it is depressed with its key :--

2) : The *Thrusting*-finger is more bent the higher the preparatory raising, and it tends to unbend as it descends towards, and with, the key.

The nail-phalanx consequently remains almost vertical (perpendicular) both in the raised and in the depressed position of the finger. This verticality of the nail-joint must carefully be insisted upon with the raised finger, otherwise we shall neither attain a true thrusting-touch, nor real brilliancy.

3) : The *Clinging*-finger becomes more open, the higher its preliminary raising, and it tends to close upon the keys in descending; or it may even be applied to the key without any change from the preliminary flatter position, for the more extremely sympathetic tone-qualities.

4) : The tip of the finger, close to the nail, reaches the key in Thrusting-touch; whereas the fleshy part, opposite to the nail, does so in Clinging-touch. In Clinging-touch the flesh is consequently pressed against the nail, and it even tends to creep round the latter.

5) : In Bent-attitude, the fingers should all be nearly equally rounded. But if the little-finger is abnormally short, we may be compelled to use it slightly straighter, in spite of the consequent disadvantage for thrusting-touch.

6): Ample preliminary raising of the finger is healthy, when there is time for it, and provided we do so solely for the sake of using our fingers *freely*.     We must, however, not allow such finger-raising to become our Object, in place of key-*use*. We must also carefully avoid hitting the key, in consequence of such ample raising,     Raising the finger off the key should be avoided, when the same finger has to reiterate its note rapidly.

7) : It is upon the proper *condition* of the Upper-arm, that depends the proper *action* of the fingers in both attitudes, as explained in Part III.

The Thumb.     8) : The difference in movement between Bent and Flat attitudes is less exhibited by the Thumb than it is by the fingers.  There is nevertheless a slight *tendency* for the thumb slightly to open-out towards (and with) the key in Thrusting-touch; and for it slightly to close upon the key in Clinging-touch.

9) : The movement of the thumb arises near the wrist-end of the hand.  This may cause difficulties unless noted, owing to the fact that the movements of the other fingers arise at the knuckle.

The Fingers, in     10) : In Hand-touch (Wrist-touch), the required Hand-Touch.     fingers should assume their depressed condition relatively to the Hand, *before* the latter descends.  In rapid passages the required fingers " remain behind," as the hand rises from its preceding notes.

Finger-Stac-     11): The return (or rising) movement of the cato.     finger differs in Staccato, in strict correspondence to the respective difference between the Thrusting and Clinging *conditions* of the finger and arm during the act of key-descent.

In Thrusting-touch, the front two phalanges of the finger rise from the key into exactly the same bent position they started from, before descent.     In Clinging-touch, on the contrary, these two front phalanges *continue* their folding-in movement *slightly beyond the moment* of Tone-commencement; the necessary rebound of the key being assured by allowing the *knuckle-phalanx* to rebound at that moment,—just as happens in the bent-finger form of Staccato.[1]

[1] *Vide* Fig 17 for Clinging-touch Staccato, page 112 of this work.

H

Fingers, Hori-       12): Seen from above, the fingers should reach
zontally Con-     the centre of their keys.   In the case of white-key
sidered.           passages the middle-finger should reach its white
key *close to the front-edge* of the black keys, the remaining fingers
reaching their keys slightly behind this position—slightly nearer
the outside edge of the key-board, each finger according to its
*relative* shortness.[1]

13) : When the fingering-position requires the thumb on a
black key, we must consider the edge of the black keys to form
the limit of the key-board for the time, and the other fingers
must, if required on the white keys, reach these *between* the
black keys; and if necessary the hand must be slightly turned
to permit of this, either to the left or to the right.[2]

Thumb Posi-           14): The Thumb should have its nail-phalanx
tion.              always in a straight line with its key; unless we
                   require it to sound two adjacent keys simultane-
ously.

Key-Position.         15) : The position of each key should, whenever
                   possible, be directly derived from the position of
keys previously played.

This is a vital matter, which however will accomplish itself
automatically, provided we duly insist upon the Act of Resting,
in one of its two forms, as previously explained.

16): The act of *finding* the position of a key, and the act of
*depressing* it, should always be regarded as two distinct acts, although there need be no break in continuity between the two.

17) : Position INSIDE the key is however the most vital point
of all—the *place* in key-descent where the hammer is heard to
reach the string, the place to which all tone-making effort must
be carefully aimed to culminate and *cease*.

Hand, Wrist,          18) : FIVE-FINGER fingering positions (whether
and Finger,        complete or not) lying on adjacent keys, diatonic
Horizontally.      or chromatic, should have the middle-finger in a
*straight line* with its key—looking upon it from above.

---

[1] It is a total fallacy to suppose that the fingers must reach their keys all
in the same line.
[2] *Vide* §§ 18-22.   Also *Vide* Figs. 16 and 19, page 112 of this work.

19): THE SCALE, owing to the required passage of the thumb sideways, demands a slightly *outwardly*-turned Wrist—or *inwardly*-pointing hand and fingers, as the normal position.

20) : THE ARPEGGIO, in addition to this normally outwardly-turned position of the Wrist, as in the scale, requires slight lateral movements of the hand and wrist to enhance the lateral stretch of the thumb and fingers.

21): DOUBLE-NOTES SCALES, owing to the required passage of the longer fingers over the shorter ones, require an *inwardly*-turned Wrist (or outwardly-pointing hand and fingers) when the scale moves towards the end of the key-board natural to each hand ; a position which is reversed on the return journey.  In short : the hand and fingers must here be turned *in the direction* the scale is travelling.

22): OTHER DOUBLE-NOTES PASSAGES—arpeggi and the like, require in addition to the last, slight lateral movements of the hand and wrist.

23): In double-notes passages, we cannot transfer the Resting-weight in both of the parts forming the double progression at those points where the turning under or over of the fingers occurs.  At such point the Resting-weight must be momentarily supported by a single finger which thus acts as a pivot, while the next two keys are prepared for depression.

The Hand.       24): The hand, at the Knuckles, should be kept sufficiently well raised off the keys by the fingers, to give the fingers ample space for free action.  The knuckles should never be allowed to be *lower* than any portion of the finger, when the latter is (with its key) in a depressed condition. The knuckle may, on the contrary, form the highest point of hand and finger, especially in the case of large hands, and in the case of Thrusting-touch.

25) : There is no difficulty in acquiring this habit, provided we remember that the knuckles should be kept up by the reaction of the fingers against the keys; and provided we do not viciously force the arm down upon the fingers.

26) : The hand should be about level ;—the little finger should

keep its side of the hand as well raised as the index-finger side of the hand; or if anything, the little-finger side should be favoured. The only apparent exception is in the case of Rotation-touch, when the hand itself tilts a little from side to side.

27): Hand-touch (Wrist-touch), implies a movement of the hand during the act of key-depression. This movement arises at the wrist-joint, and is visible as a movement of the hand at the knuckle-end.

It is not necessary that this movement should exceed the distance from key-surface to key-bottom; but the hand may, like the finger, play "from a distance" when there is ample time for such preliminary movement. Any such preparatory raising of the hand, must however be followed by its *falling* upon the keys, thus remaking contact without any real hitting of the ivories.

28): The fingers do not move relatively to the hand in Hand-touch. (*Vide* § 10.)

The Wrist.    29): The height of the Wrist is determined by the position of the fingers. Its normal position is usually about level with the knuckles, or slightly lower, if these are well-raised.    The wrist-level may, however, vary considerably without causing any discomfort, provided we do not confine ourselves either to an exaggeratedly high or low position of it.

Rapid octave passages are moreover usually found easier with the wrist-level slightly higher than the normal.

30): The wrist must alternately rise and fall, slightly, when a passage requires the thumb on alternate black and white keys. In this case the wrist is lower for the black key than for the white key. But the movement should not be greater than will just suffice to enable the Elbow to remain quiet.

Wrist and Arm.    31): Lateral movements are required of the wrist, fore-arm and upper-arm, to enable us to bring the finger-tips over their keys. The larger the distance to be reached, the larger is the portion of the limb chosen, by means of which to execute the movement.

32): These lateral movements of the fore-arm and upper-

arm and their relationship to those of the thumb and wrist,[1] require very careful attention, when first learning the scale and
arpeggio.

33) : A rotary movement of the hand and fore-arm may accompany the act of touch, when the extreme fingers of the hand
are required to sound notes. This movement is then substituted
for the more usual descending movements of the finger, hand or
arm. In such "rotation-touch" the required fingers should
be placed in their depressed position, preliminarily to the act of
touch.[2]

34) : The actual height of the Fore-arm depends on the position of the Wrist. The most natural position is about level; or
with the under-surface of the fore-arm slightly higher than the
keys at the wrist, and slightly lower than these at the elbow.

The Upper-Arm or Elbow. 35) : Correct position of the upper-arm or elbow
is most important. This is an absolutely vital mat-
ter ; for it is impossible to obtain either freedom of
reach, or the free *weight* of the Upper-arm, unless the latter *slopes
sufficiently forward*, from the shoulder. The whole arm,
from shoulder to wrist, must hence be *opened-out* almost into an
obtuse angle.[3]

36) : The elbow, viewed from behind, should while thus lying
forward, be neither pressed to the side, nor should it be unduly
protruded sideways. The elbow must nevertheless freely
change its position sideways, when a passage travels to the more
extreme portions of the key-board.

Arm-Touch. 37) : Vertical movements of the arm are of two
kinds, either of the whole arm from the shoulder,
or of the fore-arm alone, from the elbow.

The beginning and the end of each phrase is usually accompanied by arm-movement.

Body-Position. 38) : The position of the body itself is mainly
determined by the necessity for having the arm suf-

[1] *Vide* §§ 18–22.
[2] We should recall, that rotary-adjustments must accompany almost every
act of touch, although mostly unaccompanied by rotary-*movement*, and therefore invisible.
[3] *Vide Fig* 20, page 112 of this work.

ficiently opened-out, as described in § 35. Sufficient distance is therefore required *between the shoulder and the key-board;* and to enable us to give this, we must sit sufficiently distant from the instrument.

This requisite distance from the key-board can be obtained in two ways: either (a) while sitting perfectly upright (or nearly so), or (b) while leaning forward from the hips—without stooping.      This choice depends upon the length of the arm relatively to the height of the body from the hips.

Height of          39) : The chair should be placed in the centre of
Seat          the instrument. Its height is determined by the height and position of the body from the hips. When the chair is too high, we are compelled to move uncomfortably far away from the instrument, to ensure the requisite distance between shoulder and key, as described in §§ 35 and 38. Music-stools are often found insufficiently depressable.

The Feet.          40) : The feet, when employed upon the pedals, should reach the latter with the ball of the foot, while the edge of the heel is placed upon the ground, and takes the weight of the leg.

The left foot, when not required upon the *una corda* pedal, should be placed further back than the right one (on its pedal) and with the sole alone reaching the ground.

Unnecessary          41) : All unnecessary movements should be
Movements.          strictly eschewed. Even those secondary movements, required to enable us to *test* ourselves for freedom, and which must be greatly exaggerated in the learning-stage, should nevertheless subsequently be gradually reduced to the smallest limits compatible with a due fulfilment of their purpose.

Main Points of          42) : The main points requiring attention in
Position-Sum-          Position, are as follows :—
mary.

a): Sufficient distance between shoulder and key, with the seat sufficiently removed from the instrument to admit of this.

b): The distinction between the two kinds of finger-movement, with the finger sufficiently bent before its descent, in thrusting touch.

c): Avoidance of the depressed knuckle.

d): Lateral adjustment of the hand and wrist to each particular passage; the hand being turned inwards for single-notes scales and arpeggi, and turned in the direction travelled, during double-notes passages.

e): Above all things, one should insist (a) that each finger is in position, and *feels* each key, *before* the act of key-depression proper is commenced; and (b), that the position in key-descent is aimed for, where key-depression culminates in sound-beginning;——so that each key-propulsion is aimed, to culminate at the very moment that the hammer reaches the string.

Subsidiary Points of importance are :—

f): Not to allow the hand to slope towards the fifth finger——unless apparently so during the movement of Rotation-touch.

g): To keep the thumb well away from the hand,—— with the nail-phalanx in line with its key.

h): Not as a rule to allow the fingers to reach the keys near the outside edge of the key-board.

j): The slight re-adjustments of wrist-height, in passages with the thumb alternately on black and white keys.

k): In Hand-touch, and Arm-touch, the assumption of the depressed position of the fingers relatively to the hands, *before* the down-movement of the hand or arm.

l): Attention to the two alternative return-movements of the finger in *thrusting* or *clinging* Finger-staccato, respectively.

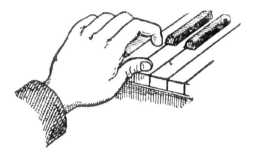

FIG. 16.—Faulty position of the thumb.

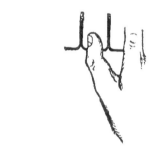

FIG. 19.—Correct position of the thumb.

FIG. 17; showing movement of the finger in *flat-finger* (or clinging-touch) *Staccato*.

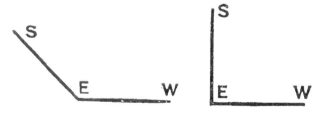

FIG. 20.—Approximately correct position of Arm.   FIG. 21.—Incorrect position of Arm.
S represents the shoulder; E the elbow; and W the wrist-joint.

## CONCLUSION.

*Glossary and Summary of the main teachings of this work.*

Part I, Intro-
ductory—the
act of playing :

§ 1. THE Act of Playing demands perception and facility in two distinct directions: (a) Musical-perception, and (b) Technical-facility.

§ 2. Musical-perception implies that of Feeling and that of Shape.

§ 3. Technique implies (a) knowledge of the requirements of Taste, and (b) knowledge of, and facility in Key-treatment.

§ 4. Key-treatment, again, has two aspects (a) Knowledge, or perception of the instrument's requirements, and (b) knowledge of, and facility in muscularly fulfilling these.

Part II, Instru-
mental aspect
of Key-treat-
ment:

§ 5. Tone-production can solely be wrought by causing the key to move.

§ 6. Loudness depends purely on the degree of speed attained by the key during its descent.

§ 7. Beauty of tone depends on our inducing this key-speed as gradually as possible.

§ 8. Opportunity for causing or influencing tone, absolutely ceases the moment the hammer reaches the string and rebounds therefrom.

§ 9. This moment, the beginning of the note (the moment of transition from Silence to Sound) must be listened for, so that our propulsion of the key can be accurately aimed to it.

§ 10. The key, in the shape of weight and friction, offers resistance to movement.

§ 11 The energy required to overcome this resistance,

varies with different keys, and with the speed at which we try
to impel them

**Part III, the Muscular aspect of Key-treatment.** § 12 We can only gauge key-resistance, by physically feeling it through the muscular-sense, before and during Key-depression.

§ 13 The act of *Attention* during performance is dual, since it implies attention musically and attention instrumentally We must listen inwardly and outwardly, so that we hear what should be, and so that we also hear the actual result; and we must meanwhile constantly *feel* the giving-way point of the keys, so that we can gauge the necessary efforts.

§ 14. Since the key must be reached so carefully, the contact should never be in the form of an actual blow, unless accuracy as to notes and expression do not matter.

§ 15 The act of Touch is consequently a Duplex process—excepting in the case of *ppp*-Tenuto or Legato :—

It consists of the two acts (a) of Resting, and (b) of Adding Energy to the key to move it.

§ 16 The act of Resting (which is continuous during each phrase) may either occur (a) at surface-level of key-board, or (b) at bottom-level of key-board.

This slight difference in Resting-weight constitutes the difference in Basis between Staccato and Tenuto, or Legato.

§ 17. The first (or lighter) form of Resting does not assist key-depression. The second (or heavier) form does;—being slightly heavier, it suffices to overbalance the key into deflection

Both forms of Resting serve to tell us where the keys are, and their resistance.

§ 18 The absolute *pp* is obtained by employing this second form of the Resting, unassisted by any Added-impetus

§ 19. The Added-impetus (Energy momentarily applied to the key during descent) is meanwhile required in all touches (except in *ppp*-Ten. or Leg.) to induce the requisite tone-amount and quality.

§ 20. This Added-impetus must absolutely cease to exist at the moment that sound-emission begins,—in Legato as well as in Staccato

§ 21. The Added-impetus can be muscularly provided in the following three forms of Touch-construction or formation —

*1st Species :* Finger-exertion alone, with passive hand and self-supported arm.

*2d Species :* Hand-exertion behind the finger, with self-supported arm.

*3d Species ·* Momentary lapse in arm-support, behind the hand and finger exertions.

§ 22. The Muscular-components which provide the Act of Touch are therefore (a) Finger-exertion, (b) Hand-exertion, and (c) Arm-weight.

§ 23 The sensations of correct touch are hence always UP-WARDS—upwards by reaction from the key, against knuckle and wrist.

This, because we can only positively *feel* the actions of the finger and hand, and not the operation of arm-weight, since the latter is derived from *lapse* in muscular-exertion.

§ 24. Movement during key-descent, depends on which of these three components is slightly in excess of the other two at the moment The resulting distinctions of movement are termed : Finger-touch, Hand-touch and Arm-touch.

§ 25. The third Species is available in either of two Sub-genera: either as " Weight-touch " or as " Muscular-touch." This, because the combination of ·the three touch-components may, in this Species, be *started* either (a) by Weight-release—that of the arm, or (b) by Exertion—that of the finger and hand.

The first makes for roundness of tone ; the second for brilliance and even hardness.

§ 26. Hardness or harshness is bound to ensue if we apply arm down-force to any appreciable extent, and when we apply our efforts *too far down in key-descent.*

§ 27. We should therefore be careful always to play " only to the sound."

§ 28. Quality of tone is moreover influenced by the two diverse Attitudes of the finger and upper-arm, respectively termed, the "Clinging" and the "Thrusting."

The first helps towards sympathetic (and carrying) tone, the second towards brilliant (and short) tone.

§ 29 It is the condition of the upper-arm (or elbow) that determines in which of these two ways the finger shall act.

§ 30. Most of the finger's work must be done by the Knuckle-phalanx; this applies equally in clinging and in thrusting attitude.

§ 31. To obtain the most sympathetic effect, we must provide key-descent through the co-operation of the clinging attitude with the third species, in the latter's weight-initiated form.

§ 32. Arm-weight, when employed in the Added impetus, must automatically cease its operation—in response to the accurately-timed cessation of the up-bearing stress at the wrist-joint.

§ 33. The transfer of the Resting weight should likewise be an automatic process, occasioned by the accurately-timed cessation of the supporting duty of the finger last used.

§ 34 Perfect freedom is imperative in all the movements and muscular actions employed in playing,—freedom from contrary-exertion

§ 35 Rotary-freedom of the fore-arm must be insisted upon, as well as horizontal and vertical freedom of the wrist-joint.                          •

Lack of rotary-freedom, especially, is one of the most common faults, since the here continually required adjustments mostly remain invisible.

**Part IV, on Position :**   § 36. The shoulder must be at such a distance from the instrument, as will enable the arm to be opened-out almost into an obtuse angle, thus enabling us to employ its Weight when required

We must be seated sufficiently distant from the instrument to admit of this

§ 37. We must distinguish between the " flat " and " bent " positions and movements of the finger, that respectively accompany the Clinging and Thrusting attitudes, and their correlated upper-arm conditions.

§ 38 The wrist and hand must constantly adjust their position laterally, so that we can easily connect fingering-positions by means of lateral movements of the thumb, etc.
The wrist must meanwhile be neither too high nor too low ; and it must change its height, slightly, when the thumb alternates between black and white keys

§ 39. The hand must be level, since the little-finger would otherwise be placed at a disadvantage. More important still, the knuckles must never be permitted to fall in, as a normal position

§ 40 The fingers should not move during key-descent, except in Finger-touch

§ 41. The thumb, in its normal position, should be well away from the hand, and its nail-phalanx should always be in the same line as its key, unless it is required upon two keys simultaneously.

§ 42. Above all things, we must always insist on being properly in position over—and even on—each key, before using it, so that Energy can be applied to it, vertically.

§ 43 Each of the keys forming a passage must not be conceived as a separate unit ;—each key's position must be conceived and must be found *as a particular distance from each preceding key,* or set of keys.

## § 44. In conclusion :

The student and teacher must once again be warned not to forget the *purpose* of Technique whilst studying its necessary details   The reminder is essential, for in studying these details, the mind is apt to dwell on *one* aspect of the problem, to the almost complete exclusion of the others.       Thus, in endeavouring to secure the visible effects of correct Position and Movement, we are apt to forget that these are quite subsidiary to those of correct Condition—the muscular actions and inactions required of us by the key, at the moment.

Again, although we may not lose sight of this more important matter, we may so concentrate our mind on the required Muscular-conditions, as to cause us to forget to apply these, accurately-timed, to the key! And even if we do not forget this, we shall nevertheless fail, unless we do meanwhile use the key only in response to the promptings of our Musical-sense,—for " Execution " itself should always be prompted by the performer's wish to give expression to his Musical-sight.

Hence, we must study the details of Position only for the sake of obtaining the Muscular-act at its easiest, and we must apply the latter only in answer to the resistance the keys are constantly offering us in varying measure And while thus muscularly judging the key, we must do so solely for the sake of the Musical-effect perceived to be necessary by our musical intelligence and feeling.

In short we must apply Energy to the key, only in strict response to what we feel is there needed to fulfil the Sound we musically wish at that moment.

A final Summary follows.

# FINAL SUMMARY

OF SOME OF THE MAIN TECHNICAL POINTS TO BE INSISTED UPON IN
TEACHING OURSELVES AND OTHERS.[1]

I. We must remember : how sound can only be made through
key-movement ; and how beauty of tone can only be obtained by
insisting upon the gradual depression (gradual propulsion) of each
key ; and how we must listen for the beginning of each sound,
if we would accurately " aim " the efforts by which we intend to
produce it.

II. We must remember : how Touch consists of the two elements, the Resting and the Added-impetus ; how the one is continuous and the other not only dis-continuous, but always as
short-lived as in Staccatissimo.        How the act of touch is
muscularly mainly built up of the three components, Finger and
Hand exertion, *versus* Arm-weight, etc., and why we must therefore always *feel* the act of touch as one of leverage upwards.
How these components can be combined into three main species
of Touch-formation, of which the *third* offers us the two great
distinctions between Weight and Muscularly-initiated touch, with
the consequent divergences in Quality of tone ; and how Quality
is further influenced by the opposite Arm-and-finger conditions respectively termed Clinging and Thrusting.        How Weight
must be ceased automatically, and how this also applies to the
act of transferring weight in Legato.        Also the great importance of insisting upon the Rotary-adjustments of the fore-
arm ; and how the doctrine of *Ease* implies perfect freedom from
contrary-exertion in all the movements and actions required, including those horizontal ones of the Hand and Wrist.

---

[1] These last Summaries are useless, unless the preceding portions of this
work have been studied.

III. How Position, whilst mainly a result, and not a cause, includes nevertheless some points of importance : such as the sufficiently-opened arm ; the difference between the raised bent and flat finger ; the lateral adjustments of the hand ; and the teaching, that every key must be felt before being played, and must be found as a lateral distance from its preceding fellow.

IV. Above all things, we must always remember that the ultimate purpose of our study is not to obtain correct Movements, nor correct Muscular-habits, but that our purpose is to obtain Command over Musical-expression.      With this purpose in view, we must, in playing, constantly *feel* key-resistance, so that we may thus be muscularly prompted to fulfil the requirements both of Key and Music.

Good tone-production can in fact be thus defined :—we must allow Key-resistance and Musical-sense to prompt us easily to move each key at requisite speed and increase of speed, to a definite Place in Time and Key-descent.

# ADVICE TO TEACHERS AND
# SELF-TEACHERS

So many enquiries having been made, how the teachings of "The Act of Touch" should be practically applied, and as to the best plan for commencing instruction in the Facts of Touch as therein described, the following advice is tendered, an outline for first lessons, which, although perhaps the best, logically, need not be strictly adhered to, and indeed should be modified to suit each individual case.

In dealing with adults, it is best to devote the first two, three (or more) lessons to a general consideration of the main principles and laws which must be obeyed during Practice and Performance if one would succeed technically and musically.

Experiment at the instrument itself, both by teacher and pupil, should constantly accompany this description and outline of these main facts. At the end of each of these first lessons, the teacher should jot down a few questions on the points explained, and should request the pupil to supply answers to these, as best he may, by the next lesson. In this way the teacher can judge how far the pupil has really understood these explanations, and the weak points can be made good.

Although the pupil cannot be expected to grasp the full significance of these explanations and directions at once, or even to remember all the statements made, yet the general outline, thus gained, of the principal laws and facts will greatly facilitate the ultimate understanding of them and *their practical application*, when during subsequent lessons they are constantly brought under the pupil's notice, as they should be.

After these preliminary lessons, the actual teaching of the

various touch methods must be at once proceeded with. Where to begin in this respect must entirely depend on the state of each particular pupil's Technique at the time; the most obvious faults being first taken in hand [1]

These practical lessons in Touch should largely consist of explanations of the pupil's particular difficulties as to Key-treatment,—muscular, instrumental, or both. Understanding these difficulties, he will then be in a position to start forming and enforcing the particular muscular-habits which will lead to correct Key-treatment, and will be able to master each difficulty in turn,—be it of AGILITY, TONE, or DURATION.

Exercises, Studies, and Pieces best suited to the pupil's stage of advancement, should be selected for this purpose; these selections should contain examples of the particular technical difficulties forming the pupil's weakest points at the moment [2]

His deficiencies being thus brought home to him, one at a time, he will be only too ready to listen when the teacher points out how these can be directly overcome, by strict adherence to the particular laws of Touch concerned, the teacher taking care to urge the necessity of unremitting attention to these laws *note by note*, during every moment of Practice, until correct habits are formed; and how non-attention to these laws will cause the Practice-hour to be wasted,—by forming wrong and undesirable habits in place of the right ones.

The student's attention should meanwhile be directed to the particular paragraphs bearing on his difficulties, found in the present little work, under "Directions for Learners" and in the "Extract", and, if he be sufficiently earnest and intelligent, to the further study of the matter in "The Act of Touch"

---

[1] Further remarks on this subject—the Order in which to study the various touch-methods—are to be found in *The Act of Touch* · Note xi, Appendix of Part III, from the seventh paragraph onwards; also §28, Chapter XIX.; §18, Chapter XX., and concluding chapter of Part IV, page 320.

[2] Thus, if the pupil is deficient as regards "singing" touch, a more or less easy Nocturne must be given him; while if his passage-work is faulty, we must choose a Study, Toccata, or Sonata requiring such touches, and give him Techniques besides which include his particular difficulties  The teacher must of course i       to t             als by thi means,     and sufficiently slow practi                                          habits.

itself—referring first to the "Contents" and then to the text
of its chapters.

It is also well, at every lesson, to set the pupil a few questions
on the difficulties under treatment, and to require him to answer
these from the material thus provided.

As regards Finger-exercises, etc , selections may be made
from any well-planned set, such as the old-fashioned "Plaidy,"
the elaborate "Le Rhythm des Doigts" of Camille Stamaty,
or Oscar Beringer's very sensible "Daily Practice "

Whichever set adopted should always be practised *rhythmically*, as recommended by STAMATY.—The performance of
Music always implies the placing of the notes in some kind of
Rhythmical relationship to each other, and it is therefore sheer
folly to spend hours in practising supposed "Exercises" while
all the while losing sight of this, the most important element
in performance—and thus *unlearning* to attend properly.  To
practise such Exercises, Scales, and Arpeggi "in rhythm," does
not mean that they should be practised *with accents*,—that
might even prove harmful under certain conditions, on the contrary, they should be practised perfectly *evenly*, but consciously
divided into rhythmical groups of two, three, four, six, or
eight notes; changing, from time to time, from one kind of
division to another, while keeping the main pulse unchanged as
to Tempo.  It is also useful, in addition, to practise Techniques
in *uneven* rhythmical figurations, such as:—

doing this with sufficient but not exaggerated accentuation.

Such training in Time, and in its subdivision, is absolutely
essential if we would learn to play musically.  Accuracy of
perception in this respect also plays a strong part in the acquisition of *individualisation* of finger.

Too much time must however not be devoted to such exer-
cise-practice.  The interminable strumming of finger-exercises,
etc., formerly considered necessary, was for a widely different
purpose  As there was no knowledge then available of the

required muscular and instrumental operations, the only course
was to make the student practise masses of such exercises, in
the hope that he might sooner or later stumble upon the *correct
ways of playing,*—hence the legions of "Methods of Studies"
extant.[1]  Such wasteful practice should now be discarded in
favour of a relatively small number of such Exercises and
Studies, judiciously chosen to exemplify in a concentrated form
the principles of Touch involved in the mastery of the various
difficulties met with.  The purpose being to enable the student
to give his whole mind to the conquest of each difficulty in
turn—a far better way than if such difficulties were casually
presented to him in the course of a musical work.  Such Exercises and Studies must also be practised for the sake of gain-
ing ENDURANCE—a very important item.  It cannot however
be impressed too strongly upon the student, that his steadfast
purpose in practising (not only such Exercises and Studies,
but Pieces also) should always be· to *learn to apply* the laws
which he has learned govern Ease and Accuracy in performance,
and never to allow this purpose to be lost sight of—nor his
practice to deteriorate into a mere *automatic sounding of notes.*

Indeed, one should never allow a single finger to sound a
note, without its musical (and rhythmical) purpose being kept
in view,—nor without keeping in sight the laws of technique
by which alone success becomes possible.[2]

Technical-practice, when thus closely directed to the fulfilment of these laws at every step, becomes astonishingly fruit-
ful, for progress then remains unchecked throughout the practice-hour

This careful supervision of the Muscular-act must not in
the least be relaxed until good habits are well-established,
and even then, attention to them is desirable in a measure,—
lest we should revert to previous faulty habits

Meanwhile, the student must be constantly urged to attend

---

[1] *Vide* the note at the bottom of page 227—"The Act of Touch"

[2] *Vide* remarks as to Musical Attention, further on, under the treatment of
children   The same remarks apply to adult-students , only in rare cases have
even the ... ... ... look for Musical shape , phrase sense, etc.

to MUSIC itself—and to do this through Attention to the KEY. Not only is this necessary during the first stages—when learning new Touch-methods—but it is necessary ever afterwards, even when the Artist-stage is reached. For we find that even those most gifted musically are at times liable to *forget* to use their musical-imagination and judgment; and are besides always prone to forget to attend *instrumentally,*—to forget to attend to Key-resistance through the Muscular-sense, and to the Beginning of sound through the Ear; omissions (the last two especially) which instantly impair the musical effect of the performance.

This last point cannot be urged too strongly upon Teacher and Pupil,—that it is only through attention to his instrument that a performer can attend to MUSIC.

Coming now to the treatment of children: Much the same course should be pursued with them as with adults. With an intelligent child one need not hesitate to start with a recital of the facts to be learned, even as advocated for adults  Of course this must be reduced to the simplest and barest outline; the teacher being careful to draw attention rather to *what has to be done,* than to the explanation of *why* it has to be done, for a child cares not to know the Wherefore so much, as the *How*-fore! Every intelligent child will indeed be found quite interested to know "the rules of the game" before starting to play; much therefore depends on the way these matters are presented;—one can only expect the child to be interested, provided the teacher makes plain the *immediate* and *practical* application of these rules.

And here, again, the moment the child essays to touch the instrument, tendencies towards some fault or other will at once manifest themselves to the alert teacher, and will thus give him the desired opening from which to start the whole chain of instruction. But before a child (or adult, for that matter) is permitted to touch an instrument, the teacher must insist on a clear understanding of the nature of the first principles of PLAYING itself,—*how* the pupil must attend (and *intend*) musically: It must be made clear, that playing consists of the combination of two things: (a) Perception of what is musically required of each note at the moment of playing it, and (b) its physical Fulfilment. Moreover, it must be made clear, that we must acquire such Musical-judgment by learning to under stand Music, not merely emotionally, but also *as to its con struction;* that is: we must learn to see how the piece we wish to play is built-up,—its general Shape, and its rhythmical con struction, down to the minutest details. We must learn to perceive what the Music *does,*—where it is that each idea, phrase, sentence, and section has its natural climax or crisis. Such understanding of the actual *material* of the music, will also enhance our perception of the musical *feeling* underlying these Shapes. For this reason, it is wrong to permit even a child to sound notes without some *musical* intention. This applies even when a child has to sound, say, merely three notes in succession. These must not be sounded meaninglessly. On the contrary, they should be *thought* as a musical "shape" or sentence.[1] Thus the following three notes may be perceived to consist of a pro gression of two notes *towards* the third and chief one, for the implied harmonies suggest a half-close:—

Even finger-exercises and scales, etc., should be thus treated; and although not necessarily accented, they should always be felt to be *musical progressions;* that is, as notes progressing *towards* rhythmical landmarks, towards the key-note here, for instance:—

In this way, the beginner will start with correct notions, realising that his endeavours must always be *musically pur posed,*—that every depression of a key must be done for the sake of Music, and that keys must never be depressed merely for the

[1] A musical phrase or sentence may be defined as a succession of notes rhythmically progressing toward a climax in the shape of *a definite point in Key,* or Tonality.

sake of making Sounds, or for the mere muscular-enjoyment of doing so.[1]

Teachers, who may find it difficult to plan out the suggested "Introductory Lessons" in logical order, will find a scheme of such lessons added to "The Act of Touch" in its second Edition. This scheme naturally falls under the following headings.—

I) How the key must be used.

II) Why true Musical-expression remains impossible unless attention is given to Key-resistance and Sound-beginning.

III) The Dual Conception of Touch.

IV) How the Muscles must be used,—a glossary of the Muscular-means employed in the act of Touch.

V) Allusion, incidentally, to the implicated laws of Position.

The whole ground is of course covered in the "Directions and Definitions for Learners"; and the teacher may therefore profitably ask the student to read out a portion of this Chapter at each of the first lessons, when fuller verbal explanations will suggest themselves as required, as the ground is gone over.

The Student should anyway start by studying these "Directions" carefully, and when he finds points unclear, he should refer to the "Extract," first referring to the Summaries of the Parts, and when those do not supply the desired details, to the Recapitulatories of the Chapters concerned. When still further detailed information is required, "The Act of Touch" itself must supply this.

The following are the main points to be constantly insisted upon, when the keyboard stage is reached, especially so at first, and alike in the case of children and of adults:—

---

[1] *Vide* the last part of the note "On Listening," belonging to the Appendix to Part I. of "The Act of Touch," reprinted here. (Page 35 ) In this connection, I would also urge teachers of children, not yet acquainted with the volumes, to adopt Mrs Spencer Curwen's admirable method for the young "The Child Pianist," and "Teacher's Guide"—Curwen and Sons.

## SUMMARY OF MAIN POINTS AS TO TOUCH, TO BE INSISTED UPON WHILST TEACHING.

a): Attention to the fact that tone-amount depends solely on the speed attained by the key during its descent.   While—

b): Beauty of tone depends on the *gradual* attainment of the required swiftness in key-descent.

c): That *correctness* in expression (correspondence of tonal-result with that intended) depends on applying one's work in answer to the key's resistance, and *before it is too late to do so,* while—

d): Agility and Staccato depend greatly on this same law being fulfilled—the avoidance of forcing the key upon its bed. Whence also we derive:—

e): The " two laws of Agility "—and of Staccato:

I): Accuracy in aiming and ceasing all Energy (intended to create sound) the moment that tone is reached in key-descent,—and which does not preclude the application of the Legato-element when required; and

II): Self-support of the arm, to enable this to be done,— the arm supported in a balanced condition, off the fingers and keys.

f): The avoidance of all key-hitting or tapping; while nevertheless insisting upon ample preliminary movements towards the keys, when the tempo of the passage admits of such, and when this is found helpful in individualising the fingers.

g): The use of Weight, instead of exertion, when singing tone is required; and—

h): The related contrasts in the finger-methods employed respectively in singing-touches and brilliant passage-work.[1]

i): Attention to the constantly-required *rotary* adjustments of the Fore-arm and

j): A few obvious points as to Position; such as sufficient distance from the keyboard at all times; the greater curvature of the finger the more pronounced its preliminary raising in thrusting-touch; the position of the hand sideways and as to the height of the knuckle, etc.

[1] Th... ... ... ... ... of the the... main Sp... res of Touch-formati... ... ... ...

# APPENDIX.

## *LEGATO FIRST, OR STACCATO?*

The question is often asked, should one teach Legato first, or Staccato?

There can only be one answer to this question, once we have really understood the first laws of Touch.  For we find, that the energy required to produce tone, if properly directed during key-descent, must NEVER be applied longer than in the shortest *Staccatissimo*, except in the absolute *pp*-tenuto or legato—when the tone-producing energy consists of the unaided " Resting " itself  Staccato, properly executed, consequently offers us an unfailing guarantee, that we have *not* prolonged the action required for tone-production *beyond* the required moment, for we cannot obtain a true Staccato (by rebound of the key) unless we do cease the energy applied during key-descent early enough.  Once we have learnt to apply the tone-producing energy thus accurately enough to admit of the rebounding-key Staccato, it is easy subsequently to change this into a Tenuto or Legato, by simply accompanying this accurately timed tone production by the heavier (Legato) form of the " Resting " in place of the lighter (Staccato) form of it

In teaching such Staccato, we must of course be careful to avoid all pulling-up of the fingers and hands—as so often fallaciously taught, and we must be careful to fulfil the law of Staccato-resting—with the hand lying so lightly and loosely, that the rebounding key can bring both finger and hand back to the surface-level of the keyboard after each short-lived act of tone-production

If it is found difficult at once to provide this Staccato form of the " Resting ", we may start by teaching the " Resting " *without* any " Added impetus ", and in its slightly heavier form, as required for Legato; and having acquired this form, and its transference from note to note (in *pp*-legato), we may then proceed to the Staccato form of it, showing how this can be transferred from key-surface to key-surface *without* any actual sounding of the notes  Having acquired the Staccato-resting, thus without any sounding of the notes, we can then successfully add to this, the short-lived act of key-depression which produces the sound in Staccato—and in all Legati beyond the *pp* tone-amount

It stands to reason, however, that before a child can be taught the somewhat complex muscular differentiations between Legato and Staccato, or for the matter of that *any* correct form of " Touch ", he must have mastered (at least to some extent) the more elementary muscular-discriminations between one finger and another  This can however often be done more profitably at a table than at the Piano itself  For no child should ever be allowed to attempt to sound a Piano-key without understanding at least those first " rules of the key " summed up on pages 3 and 4, he must at least start with a clear understanding of the simple fact that it is only by creating key-*speed* that he can create sound.

Moreover, before he is allowed to attack even the simplest tune, it must be with the knowledge that Rhythm is the supreme thing, and that he must try to make musical sentences (by means of rhythm, in the sense of accentuation) and must not merely sound successions of notes without such life being given them.

Lightning Source UK Ltd.
Milton Keynes UK
UKHW050138070223
416581UK00005B/399

9 780343 021719